JOY CHEST

Also by Jan Groft

Riding the Dog
As We Grieve
Artichokes & City Chicken

JOY CHEST

Treasures for the Journey Ahead

Jan Groft

GRAHAMHOUSE
books

This is a work of creative nonfiction. The events are portrayed to the best of the author's memory. While all the stories in this book are true, some names and identifying details may have been changed to protect the privacy of the people involved.

Published by Graham House Books
Lititz, PA
Copyright ©2018 Jan Groft
All rights reserved.

No part of this book may be reproduced, stored in a retrieval system, or transmitted by any means, electronic, mechanical, photocopying, recording, or otherwise, without written permission from the copyright holder.

Scriptures marked NLT are taken from the HOLY BIBLE, NEW LIVING TRANSLATION (NLT): Scriptures taken from the HOLY BIBLE, NEW LIVING TRANSLATION, Copyright © 1996, 2004, 2007 by Tyndale House Foundation. Used by permission of Tyndale House Publishers, Inc., Carol Stream, Illinois 60188.
All rights reserved. Used by permission.

Design and composition by Groft Design
Cover design and illustrations by Groft Design
Photography by Katherine Groft

ISBN: 978-0-9842306-2-4

First Edition

For

Darcy, Katherine, Ruby, and Macy

Table of Contents

One	The Case for Joy	1
Two	Choosing the Chest	19
Three	Relationships Matter	29
Four	A Moment in Time	57
Five	Travel & Leisure	67
Six	Faith & Inspiration	79
Seven	Home & Work	95
Eight	Creativity & Art	111
	Notes	128
	Acknowledgments	129

"Time buries treasures such as these unless you save them."

—Debbie McChesney

CHAPTER ONE

The Case for Joy

"Joy is not in things; it is in us."
—Richard Wagner

Joy is a journey we can choose to take, and this one begins with a whimsical drawing of a cat—black with white stripes and fetching green eyes. The feline is perched on the polka-dotted cover of a coloring book inspired by Gabriella Denton's folk art. It beckons me on an otherwise uneventful day near the exit of The Framery where I've just dropped off a piece to be framed. Time is short, but I have to take a look. Soon page after page of the enchanting artwork—in outline form—lead me back to a simpler time, as I recall the vivid Crayolas standing shoulder to shoulder in their yellow and green box, the magical shading from the side of a peeled-back crayon, the whiff of fresh wax and a bee-line focus that made everything else disappear.

The coloring book's pages are inviting, welcoming me to emulate the Denton originals depicted in full color on the inside covers or else splash on my own chosen hues. It would be a therapeutic funfest.

Then reality pokes in its ugly nose. My newest book has just been released. There are readings to be done, workshops to plan, emails to answer, and myriad details clamoring for attention. When would I have time to, of all things, *color*? My impulse is to pull out my wallet, but practicality says *Get serious*. I return the temptation to its shelf, hoist my purse on my shoulder, and exit the store.

By the time I arrive at my car, I am thinking, *Well, maybe not now, but how about in the future?* The plights of various elders I know come to mind. A hundred-year-old hospice patient who is alert, conversant, and unable to figure out why God is keeping her around for so long, complains of being bored. An eighty-seven-year-old divorcée who lives alone in her home of thirty-some years has often shared that she is lonely. Still another, in her nineties, relegated to her house because of medications, misses the freedom of driving and the vibrant lifestyle she once led. If not at this moment, chances are that someday—next month, next year, a decade from now—I will welcome opportunities that now seem frivolous. The more I think about it, the more I recognize that it isn't so much the thing—the coloring book itself—with which I'm enamored, but the part of me that it promises to unleash—a freer self, unencumbered by worldly distractions. I return to the store, shell out the $7.95 plus tax, and leave again, inspired.

As I drive home, images of my future begin to unfold. I've recently turned sixty-four, thankfully healthy, but what if someday I end up alone in a nursing home? Or even in a cozy little cottage where impairment might keep me from driving? Would anyone ever guess that I'd like to have a coloring book? I expect that, like most elders I know, I won't want to impose on the kindness of others to fetch things for me. What else should I think about packing for my unknowable journey? What other things aren't just "things" to me, but reflections of who I am and what I care about?

As my car inches along traffic on Fruitville Pike, a list materializes in my mind. There are the "First Thirteen Years" DVDs that my husband and I produced for each of our daughters' thirteenth birthdays, safeguarding memories of their arrivals, their precious first steps, the dawning of teen years, and everything in between. There's an autograph book from elementary school whose pages are scribbled with reminders of childhood relationships ("I love you so much, I love you so well," wrote an older sister, "if I had a peanut, I'd give you the shell"). Oh, yes, and CDs of interviews I conducted with my late father in the 1980s, bringing back his steady voice, the warmth of his laughter. There's that knitting pattern of the cowl neck scarf I made in the favorite colors of each of my daughters and granddaughters. And definitely the award that my then-first-grade granddaughter created, featuring a hand-drawn blue ribbon and captioned, "Gram: #1 Hero because you give me lots of hugs."

As items continue popping into my mind, a sense of joy captures my heart and curls up there. *I'm going to do this. I'm going to gather icons whose meanings reflect the joys of my lifetime.* Not that I'm certain of the whereabouts of all these things; I'll have to do some digging. Oh, but what a treasure they will make.

Collections with purposeful meaning are certainly nothing new. Take the Toy Chest, for example—a trunk-sized box with or without a lid, filled with objects meant to engage the imagination. Early on, Mr. Potato Head, Jack-in-the-Box, building blocks, a decked-out doll, Tommy Tonka truck, and other sundry playthings provided hours of education and entertainment.

Or think of a Hope Chest stocked with linens, trivets, flatware, candlestick heirlooms, and Grandma's hand-knitted afghan, lovingly assembled in anticipation of wedding bells and a grown-up place to call home.

At some point in life, the tangibles grow less important. Instead, experiences, relationships, wisdom, memories, interests, beliefs, and values take their place. We may have discovered that giving feels a lot like receiving. Or that the best place to be is together. Or, as the old axiom goes, that less is more. Some of us have also become more spiritual in outlook, more aware of nature, more focused on authenticity, or achieving the potential of who we were meant to be.

"The closer you come to your core," said musician and author Torkom Saraydarian, "the greater is your joy."

Wouldn't it be nice if the click of a latch helped us access our deepest delights? What if reminders of that which matters most to us accompanied us like a favorite piece of luggage as we journey from now into the future? That is the beauty of curating a collection of keepers—a Joy Chest, so to speak, celebrating the joys of a lifetime. Like the Toy Chest and the Hope Chest, a Joy Chest speaks to the heart at a new and glorious stage of life.

A Joy Chest is not some pie-in-the-sky hope to erase the challenges of aging. It is a place to which we can return—in later years or sooner, as often or as sparingly as we like—to trigger heartfelt connections. The "keepers" we choose to safeguard are simply symbols. Some have the power to reawaken gratitude, while others call to mind personal bonds or feelings of accomplishment, altruism, or faith. Still others (like my coloring book or knitting patterns) instill a sense of calm. Unlike happiness, which is temporary and often based on external circumstances, joy is lasting. Happiness provokes outward expressions of elation, while joy brings inner peace.

Whom and what do you care most about? What inspires you? What makes your heart sing? The answers will help shape your collection, one that resonates uniquely with you. Introvert or extrovert, intuitive or sensing, feeling or thinking—there are no prerequisites, no expectations. All that counts is what matters to you.

Your own unique treasures have the power to connect you with others, as well. I think of an Alzheimer's patient I visited one day at a skilled nursing facility where I volunteer for hospice. She had no idea it was her ninety-fourth birthday or who had sent the flowers and balloons that decorated her room. A photo on her dresser showed a younger version of herself sitting on a gentleman's lap, laughing. When I asked if the man in the picture was her husband, she didn't know. Nor did she remember that she'd graduated from an Ivy League college, although she said something about a closet there and then trailed off in the middle of a sentence.

A Frank Sinatra CD sat near a boom box on her dresser.

"I love Frank Sinatra," I said.

"I love Frank Sinatra, too!" she said.

"Why don't we let Frank help us celebrate your birthday?" I offered.

She nodded, and I popped the CD into the boom box. Old Blue Eyes belted out "That's Life," and I stooped down in front of her wheelchair and took her hand.

"Happy birthday," I said.

She smiled and swayed from side to side with the music, a simple source of joy and a way for two strangers to connect.

Think of it this way. Those who are wise enough to prepare for future financial, health, living, and legal challenges invest untold hours researching, investigating, and deciding. Some even pre-plan their own funerals. Exercising personal preference and alleviating the burden on others are two reasons why. Shouldn't the same kind of preparation apply to the state of the spirit?

In addition to the Frank Sinatra CDs in the room of the hospice patient, for example, there were family photographs, wall hangings reflecting her love of sea life, a framed map of Nantucket where she'd once lived and thrived, a collection of literary classics, a handmade quilt, an array of ornate brooches each from a different gift-giver, and an antique chair with needlepoint seat. Her room was her own brand of Joy Chest, lovingly created by her daughter, I suspect, to help make her feel grounded in ways that felt familiar to her. At the other extreme are nursing home rooms that are nearly barren except for the facility's weekly menu and activities schedule. Certainly some folks prefer simpler surroundings, and I don't mean to suggest that material accumulation is a prerequisite to finding meaning. As we'll soon discover, an intangible approach can be equally gratifying.

With or without triggers, there is simply something engaging about those who remain engaged. Joyfulness attracts others, drawing them in. My friend Joyce's vitality of spirit is an example. Even as she approaches ninety, Joyce dyes her own wool for the masterpiece rugs that she weaves. She looks you straight in the eye when you're talking, as though every sentence spoken is worth being framed and hung above the fireplace. Though she wasn't a mom, I imagine that every kid in the neighborhood would have wanted to live at her house. I might be telling her about a project I'm tackling, an event I've attended or my granddaughter's upcoming visit.

"Oh, Honey," she affirms with a spark in her eyes. "That is just *wonderful!*"

Joyce also knits, needlepoints, reads, continues to learn, discusses news with insight and wisdom, and fits seamlessly into outings in which my friends and I—all more than two decades her junior—are eager to include her.

On an afternoon visit, I share with Joyce the story of my recently purchased coloring book. "I'm going to start a collection," I tell her, "a chest filled with memories and meaning that might trigger joyfulness in future years for me." Her eyes sparkle with enthusiasm.

"Oh, Honey! You *have* to write a book about this."

It's hard not to soak up her supportive spirit, but I smile to myself and dismiss the notion, certain that the content of such an endeavor would fill all of three pages. But as the days and weeks pass, the seed Joyce planted begins to sprout. Ideas present themselves in the middle of the night or first thing in the morning. I jot them down, one on a pad beside my bed, another on the back of a grocery list, another on the dry cleaning receipt. Finally, it takes a file folder to hold all the scraps of paper. Joyce's own joyfulness—one of the many things that attract others to her—has buoyed my own. Then one day over lunch at a restaurant, she encourages me even more, telling me about a saltshaker stolen from a Russian airport, an article of her own that brings back an experience she loves to remember.

More than half a century ago, when Russia had just opened its borders to American visitors, Joyce went to tour the country with friends. One particular risk-taker in the group wore a long coat with numerous pockets lining the inside. Unbeknownst to his companions, as they traveled from one location to another, the gentleman helped himself to sundry mementoes, filling the pockets of his coat.

Upon their return, the group gathered to relive their experiences, and at that reunion, the man gave each of the others one of his stolen treasures. Joyce received a saltshaker from the airport café, a vivid reminder of one of her life adventures.

This is not to advocate burglary or taking uncalculated risks, especially in today's dangerous world, but just to illustrate the variety and uniqueness of symbols that conjure memories. Her story was a gift to me, as well as to my friend in the sharing.

We don't have to reach our golden years in order to reap the benefits of a Joy Chest. I refer to the elderly only because, having worked for many years with them, I've noticed a boost in spirit brought on by their sharing of memories. But no matter our age, connecting with what means the most to us is always of value. The inspiration emanating from a Joy Chest will do so whether we open its lid tomorrow, next year, or decades from now.

The idea is to ponder what you cherish most in life and then to identify keepsakes that symbolize those sentiments. Perhaps through the years you've stumbled across your own unique keepers: the humorous photo of a loved one, now passed, provoking a chuckle, or the dime-store ring your then-boyfriend bought you, asking if someday you might like a real one. Where are they now? Curating a collection of these treasures is also a good way to safeguard them.

One of my own keepers is a Christmas letter I wrote to my father when I was thirty-five years old, enumerating in specific detail why I was grateful to call him Dad. It meant a lot to him, as manifested by the tear in his eye as I read it to him, his response—"a dad couldn't ask for a better gift"—and after he died, the numerous photocopies of the letter that I discovered among his possessions. It was a tangible reflection of a cherished relationship.

As I started assembling a Joy Chest, I scoured my home for my copy of the letter, wanting to save it forever. It was nowhere to be found—not in the storage closet or the basement or my file drawers or the box of Dad's legal and miscellaneous documents. Finally, I remembered that I'd referred to the piece in my first book, which profiled Dad and our final months together. I rummaged through a file box marked *Riding the Dog* that's stuffed with rough drafts. And there it was in a folder labeled "Chapter Two."

Had I not been curating a Joy Chest, who knows where my keepsake may have landed? Chances are that someday, on a future move perhaps or while cleaning the basement, the entire box of papers would have been sent to the shredder.

Like packing for a major trip, filling a Joy Chest can vary from the spontaneous throw-it-in-whenever-you-think-of-something approach to a more organized and thought-through system. Making a list is a helpful way to get started, so you can easily add, subtract, and select only the items that are most meaningful; this can be easier than later removing items from the chest. For those who are super organized, you can even outline your list by category.

Someone once said that each of us has four areas of life that matter most. For example, the four most meaningful categories of my own life are Family, Friends, Faith, and Creativity. Others may include Travel or Work or Art or Nature—the list goes on and on. And, of course, at different stages of life, these areas may change. Identifying your own set of four, as well as other categories that once were important to you, may help to kick off your project with these guides leading to treasures that reflect them.

Others may prefer a chronological approach, outlining phases of life—childhood, school days, college, dating, work, marriage, raising children, empty nest, retirement—and then filling in with objects that highlight each one. For others, an array of lifetime experiences—holidays, vacations, special events, work, community, church, accomplishments, losses, setbacks, volunteering—may trigger choices for keepers. Still others may choose a more random approach, jotting down ideas with no formal outline.

Curating a collection, I've found, is not a once-and-done exercise, but a continuing effort that can resume when least expected. I might be rummaging through recipes and stumble upon one handwritten by my late sister, the penmanship as tidy, petite, and well proportioned as she was. Strawberry Jell-O salad: a reminder of my sister Dee. And then suddenly I'm also remembering her flawless, homemade gravy, the hours we spent chatting at her kitchen table, her sarcastic quips that made me laugh. The handwritten recipe is a keeper, not because of its utilitarian merit (though it does produce a delectable favorite), but because of its power to bring my sister back to me.

Or I awaken one morning and remember how my older daughter, as a child, used to play "mail lady," delivering letters, complete with hand-drawn stamps, through the slot in my office door. Now that she has daughters of her own, they'd seem even more precious. In which box, I wonder, did I store them?

Or I open my car's glove compartment, looking for the driver's manual, and there are two stickers that my younger granddaughter gave me one day when I picked her up from pre-school. I can still see her leaning forward from her car seat, offering the treasures. Her young voice was eager.

"Gram, these are for you!"

One sticker says, "Awesome!" The other says, "Sweet." What a blessing to rediscover something so small and yet powerful enough to bring back the sweetness of a four-year-old!

And so, let the treasure hunt begin. Expect the gathering to be diversified in nature: you might pinpoint items carefully tucked away, search for those stored who-knows-where or unexpectedly happen upon others. Depending on your degree of organization, your search will likely take on a shape of its own. Enjoy the process, remembering that a Joy Chest needn't be packed in a day. The pondering, the search, and discovery are all part of the fun. There are no right or wrong selections, but if you'd like inspiration to jog your imagination, you've come to the right place.

In an effort to offer ideas from a variety of perspectives, I reached out to dozens of friends and family members and, by extension, to their connections. I asked them to imagine a chest holding treasures that they value, not because of their price, but because of their personal meaning. Examples of "keepers," I wrote, might include a poignant letter received or a copy of one sent, a memento that made them feel appreciated, a recording or photos that bring back memories, a favorite book that continues to inspire them, a project or hobby that engages and fulfills them, a reminder of an achievement that led to a sense of accomplishment, or a token of their faith. The possibilities are endless, I conveyed, and each of us knows best which ones mean the most to us. The question I asked was this:

If you were to create a collection of cherished items to rediscover and relish over and over again, what would you choose to include? And why are those objects—those connections to your past—so important to you?

The answers were unique to the individuals sharing them, yet the accompanying tales illuminated commonly held values, such as Relationships, Travel & Leisure, A Moment in Time, Faith & Inspiration, Home & Work, and Creativity & Art. In the coming chapters, we'll explore personal triggers in each of these categories as inspiration for collections of our own.

In addition to helping shape this book in a way that would not have been possible without their unique perspectives, the respondents' stories provided something I had not anticipated: a deepening of the connections I had already felt with them or a blossoming of new ones.

As the Frank Sinatra CD in the room of the Alzheimer's patient hinted, the qualities of life that we cherish, when shared, have the power to connect us as human beings, soul to soul. And so, through a letter written to a dying friend, a birth certificate revealing a sixty-year-old's true identity, the remembered lyrics of a Welsh lullaby, and many other symbols generously shared by family, friends, and acquaintances, this book's contributors have inspired me. I hope they will do the same for you.

When we learn what matters to someone else, we gain a deeper sense of who they are. It is as close as we come, I think, to experiencing the beating of another person's heart. If you feel encouraged to assist someone else in creating a Joy Chest, I believe you will find this to be true as well.

In the same vein, imagine the legacy of your own collection when left behind for future generations. An excerpt from Official Cowboy Poet of Texas Red Steagall's book *Ride for the Brand* illustrates the priceless value. Here are a few verses from his poem "The Memories in Grandmother's Trunk."

> There's the old family Bible, yellowed and worn.
> On the first page was her family tree.
> She'd traced it clear back to the New England coast
> And the last entry she made was me.

I unfolded a beautiful star pattern quilt.
In the corner she cross-stitched her name.
I wonder how many children it kept safe and warm
    From the cold of the West Texas plain.

Life on this planet is still marching on
And I hope that my grandchildren see
My side of life through the trinkets I've saved
The way Grandmother's trunk does for me.[1]

CHAPTER TWO

Choosing the Chest

"Beauty is whatever gives joy."
—Edna St. Vincent Millay

The sky is a mid-May flat gray as Paula and I drive home from Ocean City. The two of us plus another friend spent the last three days at Paula's beach house needlepointing and talking, walking and talking, eating and talking, biking and talking, plus binge-watching and talking between episodes. Somehow our return trip is still lively with conversation.

I decide to share the Joy Chest idea with her—test it out, in a way—as she steers along New Jersey roads familiar to her. She listens intently, nods, and then jumps right in.

"I know exactly what I'm going to use for my Joy Chest," my friend says in a generous display of solidarity.

She describes a trunk that she's had since she was eight or nine years old. Her mother gave it to her, having used it herself as a little girl to hold doll clothing. It came complete with dolls, clothes, and a miniature bed. On the trunk are stickers representing the ships upon which her mother, now deceased, had traveled as a child. Born in Canada, her mother also lived in China and Nairobi, and traveled back and forth to London to visit a British grandmother.

"All these different ships that she was on treated her doll trunk as they treated regular trunks," Paula says. "They put little stickers on, I guess to amuse her. The stickers really made it special to me. I've always loved it."

Paula's maternal grandparents divorced in the early 1930s when her mother was nine or ten years old. Her mother's final London trip in which she was accompanied by both parents was marked by one of the stickers.

For some people, like Paula, a piece rich in family history lends itself to holding specially chosen keepers, and the choice is easy. For others, a search may be launched. If this is the case for you, it may be helpful to determine whether you are a proponent of form, function, or something in between.

Those who care about aesthetics will likely place importance on the style of the chest. I think of a former colleague who one day got a telephone call from his wife, presenting him with the idea of hosting a picnic dinner under a tree. My friend's immediate response was, "Which tree?" Not "Who are we inviting?" or "What will we have to eat?" but "Which tree?" A man of impeccable taste, he champions ambience.

At the same time, his engineering background demands functionality. This characteristic might lead to a fair amount of deliberation about size, weight, sturdiness, ease of opening, closing, and storing. Others might come across an old plastic storage bin in the basement, dust it off, and be ready to go. Like the treasures it holds, the Joy Chest is meant to suit you and you alone.

You can start searching now, or wait until your collection takes shape—and size—before zeroing in on a fitting piece. Unlike for Paula, the vessel that would serve as my own Joy Chest wasn't readily apparent. Instead, as I pulled my collection together, I kept in mind the quantity and sizes of my keepers, while recognizing a preference for older pieces or authentic reproductions.

My search started one Sunday morning among the musty smell of old furniture, antique quilts, century-old rugs, and collectibles. My husband and I were roaming the aisles of Black Angus Antique & Flea Market where I was partly looking for my own Joy Chest and partly seeking options that might inspire others. Soon I spotted a weathered brown valise with a Harold Lloyd Speedy sticker attached to the front, a dome-top trunk, an old dough box, an oversized wicker sewing kit, as well as steamer trunks in small, medium, and large. I pulled out my camera phone and clicked away.

A miniature reproduction of a tiger maple blanket chest was meticulously handcrafted, and I was drawn to it, but it wasn't spacious enough to accommodate my 8"x10" coloring book, and the $425 price tag was a bit over budget.

Randy and I continued exploring the flea market booths, examining candidates, snapping photos. When we finally headed toward the car empty-handed, he looked puzzled.

"I'm not exactly sure what the purpose of this trip was," he admitted, "but did you accomplish what you wanted?"

It occurred to me that the search itself can produce moments of joy, this one from realizing that my husband had been willing to wander along without fully grasping my intentions.

Some people might relish the process of scouring yard sales, furniture galleries, and one-of-a-kind shops for just the right piece to hold their treasures. Making a sport of the search might mean collecting photos or paging through catalogues to pinpoint preferences.

For others, simpler is better: an empty file box or a suitcase no longer needed for travel will work just fine, as will a fabric-covered storage box or an unused blanket chest. Look around. The perfect candidate may be tucked in a nook or cranny of your home.

Those who are crafty may prefer to build, paint, or decorate the right-sized container. The local lumberyard, hardware supplier, or unpainted furniture store can fuel the imagination. Those inclined toward practicality might head to the office supplies store in search of lidded plastic containers or portable file boxes.

Finally, a woven fabric-covered file box with leather trim and nail heads caught my eye. This fell in line with my theory about buying handbags, which is that you rarely find the right one when you're shopping for it; you just have to unexpectedly come upon it.

I was in Pottery Barn, helping a friend choose a rug, not even thinking about a Joy Chest. But then there it was, a vintage-looking piece offering functionality—just my style.

There's no requirement that the chest resemble that which its name implies. My research revealed that thinking outside of the box, so to speak, opens even more possibilities. In Chapter Six, we'll find a wall in Elaine's kitchen that holds her treasures. In Chapter Seven, we'll discover why Jim thinks of his home itself as his Joy Chest. In this Internet-focused age, some people may choose a digital Joy Chest, gaining the flexibility of photographically including more objects, organizing them into categories and easily adding written descriptions.

A quick review of social media accounts, such as those on Facebook and Instagram, reveals a variety of themed collections. One page reflects a devotion to preserving family history, showing sepia-toned photos captioned with colorful ancestral anecdotes. Another catalogues a housesitter's adventures, from horseback-riding through Argentina to bungee-jumping in New Zealand, as she travels on assignments throughout the world. Still another displays a retiree's passion for preparing exotic edibles.

For those interested in a digital Joy Chest format, there are also websites that offer photo storage, documentation, and organizing options, for example Photobucket, Shutterfly, Dropbox, Flickr, This Life, and Cluster, among others. This approach can be especially helpful not only for preserving old photography, but also for shooting and storing images of icons that are too big to fit into a chest, such as a sapling fir tree planted to mark a two-year-old's birthday or the coffee shop sign where you used to meet that special someone. If you choose this route, you'll want to investigate cost of storage, if any, privacy, and functions for editing and sharing.

Still others may opt for a different type of intangible Joy Chest, one as vast as the world itself, since the life they live requires traveling light.

My niece Suzanne, for example, admits, "My possessions are very few." When she decided to move onto a sailboat, she gave away her plants, her conch shell collection, her handmade mobiles. She sold her furniture, her bicycle, and her car. After watching a TED Talk entitled "The Ten Item Wardrobe," she embraced the concept of choosing quality over quantity and parted with racks of office clothes, casual wear, music festival garb, sexy outfits, and costumes.

Having learned to love life at sea, Suzanne describes gifts of nature, as well as experiences in the here-and-now as treasures that trigger joy for her. Examples include "seeing or experiencing demonstrations of love, smiles, beautiful sunsets, when gulls fly around the boat, when a turtle pops its head out of the water, a purring kitty, playing music and singing, dancing, offering yoga lessons, meditating, writing, cooking creative food to share, doing good work, sharing life with loved ones, and making new friends."

This ability to see the extraordinary in the ordinary or the practice of paying attention as a curious human being in a fascinating world can lead to gratitude, which, in itself, is a source of joy.

My friend David adds that "the mental images we

carry with us through the years can be as powerful as physical items—a place or time in our memories that we can retreat to that brings about tranquility, serenity, peacefulness."

Such is the case for another friend, Pam, an attorney for the Environmental Protection Agency. Although she was only five or six months old at the time—too young to directly recall the event—a video that her mother shot with a handheld 8mm camera is burned in her memory, she says.

"On this particular leaf-watching day," she writes in a message to me, her mother had wrapped her in a blanket, placed her under the giant hundred-plus-year-old oak tree in the family's backyard, and filmed her watching the leaves.

"My father had once tried to cut that tree down for fear its large, heavy branches would crush our roof during a giant wind or snow storm, but he couldn't do it," Pam shares. "The tree was simply too large."

What she noticed in the video was the sun splashing across her wide-eyed face, a crisp, fall wind rustling the leaves, and a tiny version of herself watching every leaf with her entire body.

"A life of environmental activism started that fall day, as I lay on a blanket beneath an oak tree."

A few years after Pam's family sold the house, the old tree died.

"Whether my sure and sturdy oak succumbed to disease or died of a broken heart because its best friends moved away I will never know," Pam muses, "but its spirit lives on in my memory and in the joy I find in nature."

No matter its form, the beauty of the Joy Chest, like a tender heart, is that which spills out of it—gratitude, memories, inspiration, a precious moment in time, connections to people and places loved and remembered. Whether it's a handed-down doll chest, a plain and simple box, or the whole wide world, once you open the lid, there to behold is the spirit that makes you who you are.

JOY CHEST

CHAPTER THREE

Relationships Matter

*"It's not about the tangible things.
It's about the people."*

—Paula P.

In a play entitled "Tradition 1A," my friend Howard wrote about his "Treasure Boxes" filled with notes and letters he's saved throughout the years. One box is filled with sentiments from family, one from friends, and another from his students. These treasures have played a significant role in Howard's healing process as he struggles with melanoma, having had more than one hundred skin cancers removed.

"Each surgery has taken away a small piece of my skin and a small part of my spirit," he shares.

"Every time a cancer is taken off me, from me, I go to the Treasure Boxes and take out a note, to put something back, to replenish me in some way."

Howard says that when he dies, he wants to be cremated and have the contents of the boxes mixed in with his ashes.

"I cherish those boxes, the notes, the people who wrote them," he adds.

Relationships matter. Perhaps more than anything else, they are at the crux of that which we hold dear. Life is full of difficulties and, at times, joy can seem elusive. But author Anthony St. Maarten offers a unique perspective. In *Divine Living: The Essential Guide to Your True Destiny,* he writes, "If we never experience the chill of a dark winter, it is very unlikely that we will ever cherish the warmth of a bright summer's day. Nothing stimulates our appetite for the simple joys of life more than the starvation caused by sadness or desperation. In order to complete our amazing life journey successfully, it is vital that we turn each and every dark tear into a pearl of wisdom and find the blessing in every curse."

Even amid the rubbles of illness, loss, grief, estrangement, brokenness, heartache, loneliness, and destitution, the human capacity to love and accept love can get us through. It can lift us up, hold us together, allow us to fall apart and feel safe. Through others, we can experience the presence of God or whatever name you ascribe to the miraculous comfort received.

My research uncovered a variety of tokens evoking appreciation of meaningful bonds, and experts agree that gratitude triggers joy. In her twelve years of research and 11,000 pieces of data, psychologist Dr. Brene Brown "did not find a single person who described their life as joyful who did not actively practice gratitude."[2]

Mothers and sons, fathers and daughters, grandchildren and grandparents, the best of friends, even—and perhaps especially—loved ones no longer on Earth; the bonds are meaningful, and the mementoes that capture them are as diverse as the relationships they reflect. Perhaps one or more of those shared here will inspire Joy Chest keepers of your own.

Grandma's Handkerchiefs

In the process of cleaning and purging, Missy came across a box of linen hankies that her grandmother had embroidered and edged in bright colors.

"They always smelled like licorice or patchouli since she used Clinique hand lotion," Missy recalls. "They also hold a special memory since she taught me how to iron with them. Really? We used to iron cloth handkerchiefs? A lost art!"

Michael's "Puppy"

Like many children, Marissa's son Michael had a favorite bedtime buddy that he cuddled while falling asleep each night. "Puppy," a soft, floppy brown toy, had been a baby gift from his godmother and, like a new furry pet, quickly claimed a spot in the hearts of the family.

When Michael, now a pre-teen, was three years old, his family vacationed at a southern California resort. As bedtime drew near at the end of an active day, Puppy was nowhere to be found.

"We looked under the bed and in every drawer and came up empty," Marissa recalls. "Michael was hysterical with sadness, and my insides were shaking."

She called the front desk, but there was no sign of Puppy in the hotel's lost and found. Eventually, she was connected with the housekeeping department where an employee promised to look, explaining that sometimes stuffed animals got mixed in with dirty sheets. Marissa decided to take on the sheet search herself and headed for the elevator. That's where she "met an angel," a hotel worker who listened to her story.

"She gently grabbed my hand and looked me in the eye," she remembers. "And in broken English, she said, 'To your son, the puppy is you.'

"I realized in that moment that Puppy is so much more than a stuffed animal, but a symbol of love in our family."

Marissa waited and waited in the lobby for a ride to the laundry building so she could search through the sheets. Finally, a man in a well-pressed hotel uniform drove up in a golf cart. There, riding at his side, was Puppy, who likely will be around for a long, long time.

A Bank Envelope

Barbara W's late father was a man of few words.

Inside a bank envelope, she keeps a rosary that belonged to him. Originally, the envelope contained forty-six dollars to symbolize Barbara's forty-sixth birthday.

Her mother had already sent a card from both of them, but on the outside of the bank envelope is a handwritten note wishing Barbara a happy belated birthday and signed "Dad."

"Rarely, if ever, did my father write me a note, so that makes it even more special," Barbara says. "Just knowing that he thought of me and wanted to acknowledge my birthday on his own in his own way is incredibly meaningful to me. It reminds me not to be fooled by those who do not say much—it doesn't mean they're not thinking and feeling."

Letters of Gratitude

On Mildred's kitchen table, a framed letter is matted in blue with a scattering of dried posies. Her youngest son, now in his fifties, wrote the slightly yellowed missive decades ago. She is eager to share his words, as any mother would be.

"I remember how you used to scratch my back every

night—you made me feel so safe and calm," her son wrote.

"I remember how you were never too busy to listen to me—you made me feel significant.

"I remember how you read to me almost every night—you opened my mind to imagination.

"I remember all the good values you taught me—they made me the person I am today ...

"You were the most important person in my youth, every goodness I have was sparked by your Love. I wanted to thank you, Mom, for every minute you spent caring for me and teaching me. I don't know where I would have learned my values or how to care for people if I didn't have you.

"You are the most caring mother anyone could have had.

"Thank you for Loving me so much."

An older son, whose letter is framed and hung nearby on Mildred's kitchen wall, includes these words: "I love talking to you! You have qualities one could sell. Humor, sensitivity, and wisdom, not to mention your compassion (which I could use more of). You always make me feel good, and I wanted to thank you."

Traditions Worth Keeping

No stranger to grief, Tony lost both parents when they were in their fifties, and later, his beloved grandparents.

"They never leave us," he contends. "They're always here, right at your side when you need them."

His late father, a construction firm owner, had taught him the trade. When Tony went out on his own in the business, he continued to sense his late dad's guidance. For example, he'd be on a job digging a foundation, trying to figure out how to set it or where to place wires.

"My dad told me what to do," he recalls, "right there in my head."

As his competency increased, he one day sensed his father's voice again.

"You're on your own now. *You* do it."

As his own sons grew older and worked summer jobs for him, Tony passed along to them the same skills he'd learned from his dad.

Likewise, the quiet, thoughtful sixty-three-year-old still finds encouragement from family letters that his late grandfather wrote every year at Christmas time. Reflecting the elder man's mantra, "You can be anything you set your mind to," the one- or two-pagers encouraged members of his large clan to carve their own paths, to believe in themselves, to exemplify faith, character, and humility.

Tony has not only saved these meaningful keepers, but he continues the letter-writing tradition every Christmas for his own family of seven children, their spouses, and his grandchildren, often quoting the very words from his grandfather's pieces that still inspire him.

A Letter to Mary

Linda H. and her best friend, Mary, shared seventeen years of love and laughter before Mary died from cancer.

"We could always be ourselves around one another," Linda remembers.

On what turned out to be the last evening they spent together, Mary sat with her legs on Linda's lap. The two friends were mostly quiet, but the closeness they'd always experienced was palpable. As Linda left that night, Mary asked her if there was anything she wanted to say to her.

"How do you even go about thinking of something like that?" Linda wondered. She and her friend had always openly expressed their love and trust for one another.

The next day, as Linda drove to work, Mary's question echoed in her mind. By the time she got to her computer, the words flowed.

"You asked me if there was anything I wanted to say to you," she began. "I didn't know where to start or even how to begin.... Your strength amazes me, your connection to God astounds me.... You have been my rock.... God was watching and said those two need to meet and help each other grow.... I love you, my dear and wonderful friend, with all of my heart... Thank you.... I really hate to say this, but you are going to miss me, too."

That night, Linda went home and called Mary to read the letter to her.

"We both went quiet and let our hearts talk to one another," she recalls. Later, Mary asked Linda to mail her a copy of the letter so she could share it with her husband, as well.

For Linda, the letter is a keeper, because it reflects the gratitude she feels for a "once-in-a-lifetime" friend.

Rose Petals

My friend Joyce exhibits an uncanny ability to rise above aches and illnesses, challenges and derailments. Other than defying political and social atrocities, I have never heard her complain. I've often wondered what inspired her bright spirit, and as we sit chatting at her dining room table one day, the answer becomes clear.

"My mother had the most tragic life," she recalls. "She never really had much happiness at all, and yet she always survived. She was a tremendous survivor.

"Her mother died when she was two. She was sent to live with her married sister until my grandfather re-married, and then she was treated like Cinderella. She wasn't allowed to go beyond the eighth grade because she had to stay home to milk the cows. When she was eighteen, she escaped the farm by getting married.

"Daddy died when he was only thirty-six, and she was thirty-four and left with four girls. She didn't even know how to write a check. She finally re-married when I was sixteen. He was an engineer and took us to Arkansas. From there, right after the war, he left to go overseas to help rebuild harbors. Mother never heard from or saw him after that.

"She just had a spirit that never quit. She was really quite remarkable."

That spirit would come to be symbolized for Joyce and her sisters by roses, their mother's favorite flower. When Joyce's youngest sister, Renna, was married, they collected rose petals, which the flower girl scattered along the carpet as Renna walked down the aisle. Wedding guests received a tiny box of potpourri-smelling rose petals as a memento.

"When Renna's son was married," Joyce adds, "his bride did the very same thing."

To this day, Joyce holds onto not only the rose petals but also the spirit that they represent.

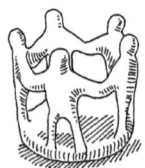

A Circle of Friends Statue

In the year 2000, Missy and eleven other women gathered to support a friend, Crystal, through her struggle with breast cancer. The group, whose members accompanied Crystal to treatments, made meals, or babysat for her two young sons, came to be known as "Circle of Friends," a name inspired by a sculpture Crystal had given to Missy. The primitive clay statue depicts a circle of figures holding hands, an apropos image for a group who joined forces and held an auction to help with their friend's expenses. The event raised more than $70,000.

"Unfortunately, Crystal died before the auction," Missy shares. "Before she died, she told her husband to ask us to continue the group and help others."

And that is exactly what the Circle of Friends did. Although emotionally drained and devastated by the loss of their thirty-nine-year-old friend, the group had money to distribute. Over the next half dozen years, they continued helping cancer victims not only through auction proceeds but also by holding an annual soup sale called "Soup for the Soul."

Performing acts of kindness or altruism has been proven by research to boost moods. Time and again, physicians and psychologists have associated these activities with people who exhibit positive emotions. For Missy, the Circle of Friends statue represents a relationship that was important to her, as well as a way of paying it forward in gratitude for their friendship.

A Telegram from Dad

My late father had a knack for motivating others, and my four sisters and I were grateful recipients of his encouragement. The first time I made the honor roll at the Pittsburgh high school to which I'd transferred, my parents were vacationing in Florida. It was the mid 1960s, long before the Internet, so I wrote them a letter to share the news. In response, a Western Union telegram was delivered to me at my oldest sister's home where I was staying. In those days, receiving a telegram was rare and typically signified an important or urgent matter.

As I read the message today, more than half a century later, I still feel buoyed by my father's belief in me. The words printed in telegraph type on the yellowed paper are: "CONGRATULATIONS. MOTHER AND I ARE THRILLED WITH YOUR BEING PLACED ON THE W.T. HONOR ROLL. BUT NOT SURPRISED. I KNEW YOU COULD DO IT. LOVE DAD."

A Mother's Signature

For years, Linda B.'s mother, an educated and talented artist, produced a variety of work, first in watercolors and then in acrylics and then in pastels and oils. But just as she'd watched her mother progress from one medium to the next, a severe case of dementia has forced Linda to face a different kind of change in her mother—this one a heart-wrenching decline into the unknown. As the severity of the disease increases, their lively and lucid exchanges are fewer and farther between.

"You live for that five seconds when the smoke clears," she shares. "And when you realize what's happened, just that fast, it's gone."

During this time, Linda has also noticed a change in her mother's signature. "She was always the one with the beautiful handwriting. Now she's not capable of signing her name anymore."

The changes have been almost too much to bear, and in the process, Linda started saving the failing signatures, "the evidence of the deterioration," she says.

"I don't know why I did. I guess it's because she's slipping away and these are the last vestiges of her," she admits, her eyes welling with tears. "She doesn't know who I am."

Linda has also saved letters. Seeing the original signature brings back the mom that she remembers.

"That's who she really is, in my mind," she asserts. "The signature that I watched her write for so many years is a tactile representation of her individuality."

Missy's Bell

As a little girl, whenever Missy was sick, her mother gave her a bell that she could ring when she needed anything.

"It sat by my bed," she remembers, "and it made me feel very safe and secure."

She passed the tradition along to comfort her own daughter, when she was growing up. The bell symbolizes a mother's love and continued support, especially when times are tough.

"Of course, it reminds me of Clarence getting his wings in [the movie] *It's a Wonderful Life*."

A Daughter's Earliest Words

After my younger daughter, now in her twenties, had just learned to talk, I found a book called *Once Upon a Child* for capturing a child's unique moments by writing down anecdotes, stories, and quotes. As the author, Debbie McChesney, asserts, "Time buries treasures such as these unless you save them."

It's hard to choose entries to share—they're all my favorites—but here are a couple from when she was three years old.

"Mommy, I think I have an ear infection in my tummy."

"We don't shoot people, because that would be derogatory."

And at the age of four, the current Manhattan career woman declared, "I'm not getting married. I'm not going to work. I'm not leaving home. And I'm not going to shave my legs."

Mother and Me

Growing up, Barbara W. recalls the impulse to make sure her mother felt loved, perhaps to compensate for her father's aloofness.

"Daddy was not the best at expressing his love for her," Barbara shares, "but, in all fairness, he got good at it as he aged, and I'm glad I now have those memories, too."

Seven years before her mother died, Barbara gave her a small book entitled *Mother and Me*. The 5" x 6" gift includes short poems and reproduced Victorian paintings in pop-up and pull-the-tab formats. On the inside cover, she wrote a note expressing what a blessing her mother's love had been to her.

"I always knew, from as early as I can recall, that she had my back," Barbara says. "Her four daughters were just the be-all and the end-all."

The gift earned a prominent spot on her parents' coffee table and remained there through her mother's waning years, including those tainted by dementia.

"As a result of her dementia, she must have sat down with the book and a pen and underlined sentences, crossed out sentences, and penned certain words in her own handwriting," Barbara shares. "Clearly, she was confused.

"It's sad that any vibrant person has to go to that place," she adds, "but I'm happy that she had the book, because I was able to express to her how I felt."

Tucked inside the book is a postcard that Barbara gave her mother long ago. It was a memento of a 1980s New York City trip that the two had taken along with Barbara's three sisters for a lunch at the Russian Tea Room. Their life at home in Lancaster County, Pennsylvania was mostly quiet with work, school, and church, and the outing was a way for the four daughters to let their mother know how special she was to them.

"We sat in a beautiful banquette," Barbara remembers, "clinked our glasses, sipped on champagne, and enjoyed caviar and blinis." A moment of joy recalled with the help of a saved treasure.

Family Tree Ornaments

Each Christmas season when I pull decorations out from storage, one of my favorites is our "Family Tree." The rustic iron sculpture has many branches for which I created ornaments years ago. Shaped like luggage tags, each decorated piece features a relative's photo, all of them together representing four generations. Every year, I hang the ornaments depicting my mother and father in a prominent spot on the tree, for they are the ones who instilled the belief in me that *family is everything*.

A Grandfather's Letter

Linda B., the eldest of four grandchildren, remembers her maternal grandfather making toys for her when she was a little girl and "endlessly reading" to her.

"I'd sit up on his lap, and I would ask him to read the same book over and over again, and without any impatience in his voice, he would say 'sure!'"

As she watched him gardening or fixing something, her grandfather taught her the importance of caring for tools, a lesson that's always stayed with her.

"He would pull the chair out for the girls in the family whenever we would sit down," she adds, "setting the precedent that this is the kind of behavior you should expect from the men in your life."

As Linda grew older and became aware of "how fleeting life is," she wrote a letter to her grandfather, expressing gratitude for all that he'd meant to her and for what he had taught her. The letter he wrote back is so meaningful that she keeps it in her bank safe deposit box.

"He wrote that of all the things he's done in life, he was proud to be my mother's dad, and that his four grandchildren have been such a joy to him that those are his proudest achievements," she shares. "It was just so heartfelt and sincere. It was not a long letter; it was concise, and it really conveyed who he was."

Expressions of Love

Barbara T. enjoys being reminded of people she cherishes via a stash of cards that she keeps in her guest room drawer and uses as bookmarks. These include photo greetings from friends and their families, birthday wishes, and even funeral mass cards.

The last birthday card she received from her late mother is one of her most treasured.

"The sentiment inside is very touching to me," she shares. "It actually makes me cry. It talks about hoping we'll be close no matter what life may bring. It's poignant, because after that, my dad got sick, and then she got sick . . ."

Another favorite is a handwritten card from her thirty-three-year-old daughter, Wray, when Barbara reached sixty, a milestone that can evoke the realization that the years are adding up.

"Dearest beautiful Mother," it starts. "I look forward to growing old with you and having a 110-year-old mother. Kind of crazy that you have another 50 years to go, huh?"

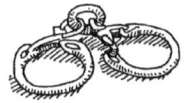

A Pair of Slave Bracelets

The tradition started when Paula P. was about twelve years old. Each year for her birthday and for Christmas, her father gave her a piece of antique jewelry, "none of it particularly valuable (my mother got the good stuff)," she admits.

Still, Paula values the gifts in a different way.

"I have such fond memories of my dad," she says. "It's something that I so connect with him."

She intends to keep a few and pass others along to family. The unique gifts include, for example, a pair of "slave bracelets," designed to resemble manacles originally worn in the 1850s and 1860s by women supporting the abolishment of slavery.

"It's not about the tangible things," she adds. "It's about the people."

Photos and More Photos

Because of the visual dimension that photographs add to memories, it is no surprise that joy-seekers cited them time and again as keepers. Whether in frames or in albums, on-line or on walls, photos can capture the essence of those we love. Paring back photographs to select favorites is worth the effort and can lead to a collection that is especially powerful and moving.

Ward thinks of a 3" x 3" black and white photo on his desk as a time machine. It takes him back to a public park near Buffalo, New York, during the summer of 1949. In the snapshot, his father—dressed in khakis, a white tee shirt, his legs casually crossed—leans against the side of his newly purchased Hudson Coupe. His hand rests on the shoulder of a knobby-kneed four-year-old wearing baggy shorts. The child is Ward standing proudly next to his father, tiny hands on hips. His family has traveled from Pennsylvania to visit an aunt.

Sixty-seven years later, the photograph brings the moment back to Ward.

"I can feel the burning heat of the metal car door when I leaned against it trying to imitate my father's pose," he shares. "I can see my mother squinting through our box-like Brownie Hawkeye camera and backing up in order to get the whole car in the shot."

He even recalls his baby brother dressed in a red and white outfit and gurgling on a nearby Army blanket.

"That small picture never fails to raise my spirits and make me smile," he adds. "It transports me back more than half a century to a time of innocent joy, a time when my parents were still alive and we were all happily together, a time when I still had my entire life ahead of me, and the whole world was bright and sunny and new."

Howard cherishes four photographs in his living room.

"On a table near a window is a sepia-tone photo of my father holding me when I was, perhaps, two years old," he says.

On the other side of the living room, a black and white photo portrays Howard's late wife holding their young daughter.

"You see unconditional trust and love in both their faces," he describes.

Above that is another black and white photo. It's "of me holding my son over my head," he notes. "And above that is a color photo of my son holding his son over his head.

"I look at those photos often, grateful for the continuity. Life from one generation to the next."

BJ's home is filled with framed photographs of family and friends representing many generations.

"Some of these people, now long gone, still look at me with a story in their eyes," she shares. "My dad in his Army uniform, my mom in her wedding dress, my grandparents at their 60th wedding anniversary, my siblings as children around our Christmas tree, my children's school pictures up to graduation, my grandchildren as babies and as they grow.

"There are old black and whites," she adds, "sepias and hand-painted photos from the past for which my ancestors sat in rigid poses."

BJ holds precious "the thousand words behind each picture" and the stories from her parents that come to mind.

"Every moment, visit, vacation, birthday, sports event, and birth are re-sealed in my memory by just one look."

In 2010, Barbara T's parents died within two weeks of one another.

"For them, it was good, because neither had to live

without the other for very long," she notes. "But for us, it was very tough."

After her mother's and father's house had been sold, she returned one last time. There she met her parents' attorney who'd discovered a photo that had accidentally fallen behind the piano. The heart-shaped frame held a portrait of her father about to plant a kiss on the cheek of her mother. The picture itself, as well as its serendipitous discovery, was uplifting.

"That was my parents' message to me," Barbara muses. "It's as if they were saying, 'We're here; it's going to be okay.'"

Linda B., a young widow, says, "An album of my wedding photos becomes more precious with each passing year, as so many who were present are no longer here."

Among her keepers, Cheryl lists: "a picture of my father hugging me at the rehearsal dinner of my brother's wedding; a picture of my mother as a girl; a picture of my husband and step kids; and lots of pictures of my dog, Gracie."

JOY CHEST

CHAPTER FOUR

A Moment in Time

"I learned a lot about my father that day."
—Patti

Patti remembers, as a young girl, tossing a baseball with her father after supper and the two of them memorizing players' statistics from the back of baseball cards. After she was grown and had daughters of her own, her dad beamed with pride as he showed off his only grandchildren every chance he got. In October 1981, soon after the birth of Patti's second daughter, her beloved father, at age fifty-two, had a heart attack and suddenly died. At that moment, she says, her world changed. Thirty-three years later, it was to change again in a way she would never have guessed.

In November 2014, a seasonal employment opportunity required that Patti submit her birth certificate, which, she realized, she didn't have. Her mother handed her a small white envelope with the original document inside and advised her to read the notation next to Father's Name. On the line was one word: "Refused."

"No worries, Mom," Patti, now sixty-one years old, assured her. "I sent away for a new one, and it will have Dad's name on it."

"He wasn't your father," her mother corrected.

Patti looked at her mother, stunned. She was speechless. She learned that the only parents she had ever known had been married and then divorced. Her mother then became pregnant by Patti's biological father and two years later remarried the man who would raise her.

As Patti listened to her mother's explanation and the name and whereabouts of her natural father, tears began to fall. She had never once felt unwanted, making the news even more shocking.

Afterward, with the help of the Internet and Patti's own out-of-town daughter, she found the contact information for her biological father. It was around 5:30 p.m. on that same day, a Friday, that Patti decided to make the call. The father she had never known answered.

"Is this Bill Yost?" she asked.

"Yes, it is."

"Do you know a Nancy Badorf?"

"Yes," he answered. "Yes, I do."

"This is Patti," she said.

A brief pause. And then, Patti recalls, his voice became all but a whisper.

"You were always on my mind."

They talked for about ten minutes.

"He told me he'd always wanted to get in touch with me but was never sure when the right time would be," Patti remembers. "He had never seen me, not even when I was born. His wife had recently died and over the last year, he'd also lost a brother, a nephew, and a niece."

Her newfound father asked if he could call her again, and Patti agreed.

"Since that day, he's called me every day and the last thing at night to say 'goodnight' and to tell me that he loves me."

A month after that initial call, the two met in person for the first time. Since then, they've gotten together as much as possible. He loves singing, Patti says, and he encouraged her to join him, "something I never had the confidence to try." They went on to sing duets with live bands, as well as karaoke. Her father's signature song: Willie Nelson's "Always on My Mind."

On a recent Memorial Day, Patti's biological father accompanied her to the gravesite of the man who raised her, offering to wait in the car to allow her privacy. Standing at the grave, she began to cry.

"Soon I felt an arm on my shoulder," Patti shares. "Dad handed me a small flag he had received as a vet to place on the grave .... He said he needed to visit the grave as much as I did. He thanked my dad for raising me.

"I learned a lot about my other father that day and realized how fortunate I was to have two dads."

Patti cites the special moments in her life that have brought her joy: her wedding day, the birth of her daughters and granddaughters. But the turning point symbolized in that one piece of paper—her birth certificate—as well as by a veteran's flag passed from one of her fathers to the other made her "appreciate what I have even more and certainly has changed my life forever."

In literary terms, the moment in a story where a character comes to a realization that changes the prism through which everything else is viewed from that point forward is called an epiphany. The Irish writer James Joyce described the moment as one in which "the soul of the commonest object...seems to us radiant...and may be manifested through any chance, word, or gesture."

Patti's birth certificate and the gift of the veteran's flag have that kind of radiant soul with the power to stir deep thoughts and questions. *Who am I? What do I mean to others? Why am I here? How does the world look to me? What is my worth?*

Special events marking a passage in time from one stage of life to another are also rife with symbols of meaningful change. Even moments that did not seem out of the ordinary at the time can, in retrospect, illuminate enchanting points of view. The following items reflect moments in time or events that were important enough to be labeled as keepers by those who cherish them.

Wedding Dress

For Linda B., her wedding dress brings back not only the beautiful November day when she and her husband, Barry, exchanged vows, but also a sense of gratitude for those who were in attendance.

"All these people who I loved were with me to celebrate," she recalls. "The only other time I felt that collection of love and support for a life transition was at Barry's funeral."

On the latter occasion, she remembers riding alone in a limousine from the funeral home and arriving at the church where all her family—her cousins from New Jersey, her uncle, her parents, her siblings—were standing outside the door.

"It was a very powerful thing. It felt like they were there to greet me," she says. "I kind of envision that's what heaven must be like, that they're waiting at the door for you."

It's been five years since her sixty-two-year-old husband died and at least that long since she's taken out her wedding dress. But still, she intends to keep it.

"If I would look at it now," she muses, "I would say, 'Holy cats, was I skinny!'"

A Newborn's Welcome

A few months after her mother died, Cheryl received an audiotape that her father had found while cleaning out a closet. He didn't know what was on it, but it was dated June 17, 1964, two days after Cheryl was born.

She had the tape converted to a CD, expecting it to contain her mother's voice, "a voice I was just learning to live without," she wrote in an essay entitled "Welcome to the World."[3] Her parents lived in Philadelphia, and Cheryl guessed that her mother, a native of South Africa, had made the recording to share with her own parents, who still lived there.

She decided to listen to the recording on Yom Kippur, the holiest day of the Jewish year, a day of prayer, fasting, and quiet reflection that her mother had always cherished. To her surprise, the first voice she heard was that of her grandfather, as he waited for the operator to put his congratulatory telephone call through to the newborn and her family in Philadelphia.

"The relief in my mother's voice when she heard her parents on the phone was palpable," Cheryl wrote. "She wearily but proudly proclaimed me a healthy, beautiful, six-pound baby girl who resembled her sister, Sandy. Hearing this, my grandfather began to weep."

On the tape, she said, there were tearful expressions of love between her parents and grandparents. There were cheers, congratulatory messages, toasts, and a South African rendition of "For She's a Jolly Good Fellow," as twenty-five of her grandparents' friends arrived at their home to celebrate Cheryl's arrival.

"Hearing the rejoicing my entrance into the world prompted was startling," wrote Cheryl. "A party. Tears of joy. Wine and song. What was next, I wondered—a marching band parading through their living room?

"I played the tape hoping it would assuage some of my homesickness for my mother, never expecting it would also assuage a deeper homesickness within myself," she added. "How astonishing to hear myself being welcomed into the world with merriment and song. What I had spent my entire life doubting—namely my inherent worthiness—was now being turned upside down with the undeniable evidence being played back to me on tape."

Marriage Proposal Take Two

The night Rick showed up at Karen's apartment to propose marriage to her, she was frazzled. It had been a rough week at work, and the pile of bills seemed never-ending. In short, she was in a bad mood. Although the timing was less than opportune, Rick decided to follow through with his plan.

In no uncertain terms, Karen conveyed the problem with Rick's timing. Her annoyance escalated when, at a party afterward, a friend of Rick's told Karen that he'd heard congratulations were in order.

Take two. The next evening, the hopeful boyfriend returned to Karen's apartment with a bottle of Mumm Champagne. Careful to make sure the mood was right, he took another stab at the proposal.

Thirty-four years later, the two of them laugh when they share the memory. And still in Karen's possession is the empty champagne bottle from the night that Rick got it right.

"It's symbolic of the start of the most wonderful part of my life so far," she admits.

A Round Stone

When Joyce's niece, Tamala, graduated from nursing school, many of Tamala's relatives, including her paternal grandfather and maternal grandmother (Joyce's mother), traveled from various distances to gather for the ceremony.

"It was the only graduation that Mother was able to go to," Joyce notes, "so it was a uniting of both sides of the family, which made it very important."

On the way to the Museum of Fine Arts in Boston, where the graduation was being held, Joyce tripped over a stone.

"I had turned around the corner too sharply, and I caught my toe on the stone," she says, laughing. "I just stumbled; I didn't get hurt. But the stone! A round stone! It's this big!" She opens her hands to about the size of a grapefruit.

She takes me to a door overlooking her patio, where the round stone now sits. To her, it brings back a day of celebrating accomplishments, as well as one of family togetherness.

"It's just a reminder of all the things we were able to accomplish to be together for that particular event," she shares. "And that was pretty wonderful."

CHAPTER FIVE

Travel & Leisure

"I always had a sense of wonder about what the world was like outside my little town."
—Karen

The autumn sun was shining on the Dallas golf course where Guy and his buddies gathered to play. Theirs is a cohesive group, getting together weekly to catch a sporting event, play golf, or travel. Now, one in the foursome, Mike, stepped up to the tee and, as he did, Guy was thinking of all the possible targets for Mike's shot. Guy says, "I'm thinking the homes to our left and right are the most likely objects in peril, not the green—last of all the green. He has days where he struggles beyond imagination with the game. A train wreck from first tee to last. But he plays on; the friendship of the group overcomes the pains of the game."

Today, however, was different. The sound of Mike's

swing on contact was crisp, the ball taking flight on a high arch in direct line with the green.

"In midflight, we're all giving him the 'nice-looking shot' preapproval," Guy remembers. "The ball lands on the green, and we're congratulating him as the ball rolls and rolls. The flag is a long way off as the ball continues across the green, and it's heading in the general direction of the stick.

"Now we are all transfixed," he continues, "watching that ball as it rolls and rolls and rolls . . . finally taking dead aim at the hole, and it's gone. Hole in one! Spontaneous combustion . . . we're screaming and hugging Mike in a moment of disbelief."

That moment lives on for Guy not only in his memory, but also, of all places, on his golf glove. Here he has scribbled words of encouragement to boost his own game. *Heads up*, for example, reminds him to keep his head still and chin up. *Load right* means to take the driver back low and slow while shifting weight onto the right foot. And the words *Magic Mike* help him summon the magic Mike showed the others that day.

"Like him, I have good days and bad days on the course," Guy admits. "And when it's going bad, it sucks. Hard to shake, and it can spiral out of control.

"He turned the worst of times into the best of times."

At the heart of Guy's story, a sportsman's delight, is a tale of friendship. Spare time and the way we spend it can lead to a treasure trove of meaningful experiences.

Travel, for example, might offer a breathtaking encounter with nature, a unique experience of history, memorable exchanges among family or friends, a moment of spiritual connection, or a meaningful time of rejuvenation. Reading can provide a sense of escape, inspiration, or connection with fellow human beings. Needlecrafts and woodworking satisfy cravings to create something of beauty, offering peace and relaxation and a chance to give from the heart. The list goes on.

The following keepers are mementoes of travel or leisure activities that are especially meaningful to the people who described them—the roads they traveled, the fun they had, the memories garnered along the way. Perhaps they'll inspire your own collection, or you might just find vicarious pleasure in the experiences shared.

Cigar Store Indian Photos

After his father died, Jim was flooded with fond memories of the family vacations they'd taken together. His reminiscence prompted the realization that he and his wife hadn't vacationed since their son was born. So a year later, in 1979, Jim, his wife, their six-year-old son, infant daughter, and Jim's mother headed together to Disney World. It was their first visit there and the start of an annual tradition that has spanned nearly forty years.

Upon that first visit, and every trip since, his kids have posed for photographs in the very same spot—next to a statue of an Indian in front of the Magic Kingdom's Main Street Cigar Store. Today the tradition continues with the couple's grandchildren.

The photos, tracing the growth of his children year after year, are a reminder to Jim of the happy and memorable experiences shared there with family, even including the weddings of both his son and daughter.

"It's a magical place that has become an important part of our lives," he says.

Travel Journals

Karen grew up in a small town near Erie, Pennsylvania.

"From the time I was young, I always had a sense of wonder about what the world was like outside my little town," she shares, "and I knew I needed to explore it."

And explore she did, living for a year in Israel, hiking the hills of the Basque region, snorkeling in St. John and

Turks and Cacaos, pitching tents amid the grapevines of Italy and the melting snow of Switzerland, and traveling to England, Ireland, Puerto Rico, Turkey, Egypt, Greece, Yugoslavia, Austria, Spain, France, and Germany.

When Karen travels, she enjoys writing about her perceptions of the people, activities, and surroundings of the places she visits. The endeavor has produced several journals, each capturing the experiences she had on a particular trip.

"When I'm old and unable to travel," she says, "I hope that my journals will be able to take me on those trips."

In a similar vein, she consumes the writing of others, whether in the form of print, digital, or audio books.

"Like travel, books have always served to open my mind to different worlds, ideas, other ways of thinking," she notes. "I can't imagine my mind not being able to have that kind of stimulation when my physical world grows smaller."

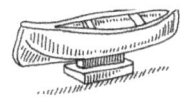

Joyce's "Sit-Abouts"

In 1935, when Joyce was in the first grade, her

teacher, Mrs. Hartzell, invited an author friend, Richard Halliburton, to speak to the class. At that time, Halliburton had penned *The Royal Road to Romance*, the first in a series of travel biographies detailing his adventures around the globe.

To this day, Joyce remembers being mesmerized as the well-regarded traveler spoke of crossing the Alps on an elephant and swimming the Hellespont. It was that experience, as well as Mrs. Hartzell's own travel photos of the Grand Canyon, that ignited Joyce's lifelong passion for exploring.

"Right then, I decided I wanted to see the Grand Canyon," she says. "I wanted to travel to all these places that they had traveled."

And travel she has. A curio cabinet in Joyce's living room displays shelf after shelf of what she calls "sit-abouts," mementoes from the places she has visited, each with its own story. For example, there is a miniature canoe handcrafted of leather, reflecting those used by Tierra del Fuego natives who would jump into the cold river naked, scooping pearls out of clams and placing them in baskets similar to the attached replica, woven of reeds and intricately detailed.

"A lady and her little girl were sitting at the wharf when we were getting back on the ship," she recalls, the memory still fresh in her mind even decades later. "She sold it to me for a dollar."

Joyce's showcase also includes miniature brass llamas from Argentina, a replica of the Lewis and Clark boat from her trip along the Snake River in Washington, a tea-maker from Uruguay, a miniature glass Delta Queen paddleboat, to name just a few. And, of course, she has saved the book that started it all, now yellowed through the years: Richard Halliburton's *The Royal Road to Romance*.

A Wooden Nickel

When Barbara T. was twenty-one years old, she decided to leave her position as a special education teacher in Michigan and head to Utah State University to pursue a master's degree. She would make the drive alone through the Rocky Mountains and west.

"Back then, that was a huge thing," she notes. "I was really scared. Now my daughter just travels all over the world, but for me it was a big deal to drive all the way from Michigan by myself."

En route through Nebraska, she stopped at a place called Johnny's Big Games located at Exit 360 on Route 80, according to the imprint on a wooden nickel she received there. Four decades later, the token still provokes the memory of her accomplishment.

"I kept it as a symbol of strength," she adds. "And if I ever go back there, it's good for one cup of coffee."

Missy's Hats

Missy loves wearing hats, and she deems a couple of her favorites well worth keeping for the long term. One is a red beret that she got on her first trip to Paris in 1986. To bring back memories of a cherished experience there, she likes to place it in a cocked position on her head of long curly locks.

"It tames my hair," she adds, smiling.

Her Kentucky Derby hat, decorated by her daughter, conjures up memories of a family trip to the Derby to celebrate her fiftieth birthday.

"It was the perfect trip with my love of hats and love of horses," she shares. "I don't have my horse anymore, but I still have my saddle that sits in the attic on a sawhorse."

Frozen Yogurt Tour Invite

My younger daughter and I enjoy sharing a variety of experiences when I visit her in New York City. One of our favorites has been a food tour of Old Greenwich Village. In fact, we enjoyed the three hours of taste treats and culture so much that we've since gone on similar adventures in other parts of the city.

Soon after we'd completed the first tour, she gave me a unique Christmas gift that reflected our experience as well as a shared penchant for frozen yogurt with all the toppings. It was a custom-designed invitation for a "Frozen Yogurt Tour" that featured a "Foods of PA Tours" logo, fashioned after the one in New York, and a list of four local "participating locations." With the invitation came four gift cards, one for each of those stores. For other holidays, she has designed coupons for a mother/daughter NYC lunch date, a hotel booking in the city for a "Girls' Getaway Weekend," and other experiences. I cherish every one of those pieces, as they reflect the most meaningful gift of all—the mother-daughter time spent together and the reminder that she values it as much as I do.

Racetrack Timing Slips

When Jim was in college, he owned a 1962 409-Chevy, "like the car made famous by the Beach Boys song," he notes. More than just an automobile to him, the "409" holds treasured memories, such as his dates with the girl who would become his wife, his street racing experiences (at which he was never beaten), and the trophies he won at the drag strip.

After his children were grown, Jim located a similar '62 Chevy and set about creating new memories when he found a professional to restore it and recreate the vehicle he remembered. In the process of directing the restoration, the man he'd engaged to do the work became a close friend.

Jim has saved some of his drag strip timing slips, a photo of the car on the day he bought it, and a photo of himself racing it at a local drag strip—all seemingly small mementoes, but powerful enough to take a man back through the decades for another spin in his "409."

A Tour Guide's Scarf

When Barbara T. and her husband traveled to Peru, they hiked to the breathtaking city of Machu Picchu, built atop the Andes Mountains. Competent, well-versed guides led their hiking group through different climate zones and up a 14,000-foot peak. One young guide from Cusco, Peru, wore a colorful, soft scarf that Barbara admired. His name was Abel, and he was the guide with whom she especially connected.

"He taught me the best way to hike downhill, because I tend to be really tentative," she notes. "I still use his ideas and techniques to this day."

It was a challenging trip for Barbara, including a bout of sickness resulting from water she accidentally drank when brushing her teeth.

"I had a fever," she says, "but I made it. I hiked and kept going."

After ten days on the trail, the group reached the train station from which they would embark for the last leg of their trip and where they would have a party to say their good-byes.

"I was really emotional," she remembers, "because it was an unbelievable trip."

Remembering that she had loved his scarf, Abel gave the hand-woven piece to Barbara's husband to give to her when they reached Machu Picchu.

"Now I'm a doula, and I use the scarf as a *rebozo* to help women when they're in labor—to support them or put around their eyes or their body," she shares. "And I use it for myself when I feel like I need strength or support."

CHAPTER SIX

Faith & Inspiration

"They remind me that while there are many different ways to express faith, we're more alike than we are different."

—Linda B.

In September 2015, my younger daughter and I traveled to France to live briefly among the Benedictine monks. I had been experiencing a long and rough period of turmoil, and Katherine, who craves travel and adventure, was looking forward to the diversion from city life. From the moment we stepped off the train in Sablé-sur-Sarthe, France, I was feeling a bit lost, which, I see now, was a manifestation of a personal relationship which had become rife with misunderstandings and heartache.

The travel agent had assured us that cabs would be lined up at the station for easy transport to St. Peter's Abbey in Solesmes where we would be staying. But on the Sunday that we arrived, we exited the deserted station into the sunlight to find only a tiny village lined with trees, one closed restaurant, and not one person in sight.

How do we find our way? I wondered.

As any informed traveler would do, we had pre-arranged for foreign cellphone service so, thankfully, we could call a taxi or, at least, the monastery. But when I dialed one number and then another, a French-speaking recorded voice, which I could not understand, left me clueless.

How will we connect?

Finally, we found a lone worker in the station's back room. It was by now apparent that my endeavor to brush up on long-ago high school and college French lessons had been futile. After a series of charades, our new friend called a taxi for us, and soon we were on our way.

The cabdriver was a petite French woman who understood not one word of English and drove like the proverbial bat out of hell. The car swerved and screeched as we tried to communicate to her that we needed to stop somewhere for groceries.

Despite the monastery's mandate to bring our own food to prepare in our assigned cottage, we had decided it would be easier to purchase rations when we arrived, as opposed to juggling them with our luggage. Little had we anticipated the extent of the monastery's isolation or the Sunday closing of the rare establishment that did exist.

How do we find nourishment?

In the end, pastries and quiche from a boulangerie got us through, and in light of what we discovered among the Benedictine monks, our troubles subsided. Steeped in a thousand years of history, the group continues their work today of restoring Gregorian chants according to ancient manuscripts so that, in the words of Pope St. Pius X (1903-1914), all people may "pray with the help of beauty."

Everywhere, sure enough, beauty embraced us. We heard it in the pitch-perfect chants sung six times daily during liturgical prayer time called "offices." We experienced it in the peaceful gardens with bowling green lawns and in the yew trees clipped into cubes and cones. We saw it in the overflowing flowerpots hanging from village lampposts. We felt it in the simplicity of our guest cottage at 10 Place Dom Guéranger and the nearby River Sarthe, welcoming us on bikes along its banks.

In the Abbey's bookstore one day, we asked a middle-aged monk, working behind the counter, where we might find a grocery store. We couldn't think of the correct translation, but through pantomime coupled with French words we knew for every food we could think of, we were finally able to communicate the place we needed to find. He sketched a map for biking there, and then he drew the same map over and over again, pressing his pen at each turn, as though repeated drawings of the same route would somehow break our language barrier. Even without that benefit, we soon felt akin to those sharing this sacred space—the quiet yet kindly monks, the hostess named Martine, the wrinkled, hunch-backed woman pedaling to daily offices, a loaf of bread protruding from her bicycle's basket.

On my second or third morning there, I awoke in my tiny, sparse room to the Abbey's chimes signaling the start of Lauds, the early office. Suddenly, the sound of the chimes made it seem as though my whole world had changed. God's presence was palpable, and the message that I sensed was this: *I am with you. Stay close to me. I will never desert you.* A lightness I hadn't felt in years filled my heart. At the moment, I had no idea that from then on, the sound of church bells would blanket me with feelings of undeniable peace.

Now in the mornings at home, Gregorian chants from CDs grace my living room. Sung by the monastic choir of St. Peter's Abbey, one of them features music from the offices of Vespers and Compline. I cannot get enough of it. The very first sound on track one is that of the Abbey's bells tolling.

As my Gregorian chant collection does for me, spiritual reminders can offer comfort and a quiet sense of joy to others. Some people keep notebooks of inspirational phrases that resonate with them. My own set of spiral-bound index cards is divided by various personal struggles I've identified—e.g., worry, busyness, letting go—and I've filled each section with verses and quotes that address these issues and help to motivate me, when needed.

Others might treasure the religious artwork of a child, affirming the passing along of tradition from one generation to the next. Still others might pray the Bible for children and others they love, jotting dates and prayers in the margins, seeking help for their needs and blessings upon them.

Symbols that provide inspiration, spiritual or otherwise, are so varied and personal that often they give the sense of having been custom-designed. Including them in a Joy Chest can calm a heart, whenever needed. Here are just a few examples.

Claire's Tear Box

Missy's husband, David, chose a small metal container and designated it as their daughter Claire's "tear box." Each time she cried, as a child, her father would quickly bring the box to her and collect her tears.

"It often made her laugh," shares Missy.

She refers to a Bible verse that captures God's comfort in sorrowful times.

The Psalmist (also named David) writes, "You keep track of all my sorrows/You have collected all my tears in your bottle."[4]

A Mom's Bar Mitzvah Speeches

When Karen was called upon to write Bar Mitzvah speeches for each of her two sons, she found it a daunting assignment.

"You feel the burden to impart some words of wisdom as guidelines for them as they enter adulthood," she remembers, "even though they might let it go in one ear and out the other." And as many parents discover when raising children, her confidence in where they were headed had occasionally been put to the test.

"It was a time to sit down and push the pause button and start at the beginning," she remembered. In her younger son's speech, that beginning was shortly after his birth.

"I was trying to catch up on some much-needed sleep in my hospital room when I heard a blood-curdling scream coming down the hall," she wrote to her son in the speech. "My first thought was 'Boy, do I pity that mother!' Well, lo and behold, *I* was that mother. The nursery nurse quickly deposited you in my arms and made a fast exit to the door with the comment, 'I've heard lots of screaming babies in my life, but this stinker takes the cake.'"

The memory led Karen to reflect on her son's self-assurance, his zest for life, his *chutzpa*. For both boys' speeches, as she continued to write and remember, the exercise brought her an unexpected gift.

"It helped me to realize how their unique strengths had blossomed since early childhood," she recalls. "In our day-to-day lives, I think we sometimes lose sight of the person they are becoming."

The glimpse into their future, she says, reassured her that they would be just fine. Today, with both sons grown and living happy and successful lives, the speeches she wrote for them have become treasured keepsakes.

"It was one of the most rewarding things I did during their younger years."

Siddhartha

"I've always been very spiritual," says Barbara T., who was raised Catholic and now considers herself a Buddhist.

"I studied Buddhism, and I meditate and go on retreats. I've been doing this for many, many years."

Having just turned sixty, she is intrigued by choices she made as a youth—such as the friendships, experiences, and traditions she held dear—and reflects on how they compare to her preferences as an adult.

"I'll sometimes wonder, was that just a passing fancy or what was I like back then?" she muses. "Am I really that different now that I've grown older?"

And what she's come to find is that no, she's not. In the realm of spirituality, for example, Barbara looks back to her high school years and recalls having read Herman Hesse's *Siddartha*, a book that had an impact on her.

"I was so intrigued by the Buddha," she remembers. "It was my introduction to Buddhism."

Since then, the Buddhist tradition is one that she's continued to embrace, and the book, now dog-eared and worn, remains a symbol of that.

"I still have that book on a table in my bedroom," she says.

The piece represents not only her spiritual beliefs but also a past and present that connect for her in meaningful ways.

A Cross Wall

When Elaine and her husband, Mike, moved from Louisville to San Antonio, they downsized from 3,400 square feet on nearly two acres to an 1,800-square-foot condo. In the process, they carefully selected treasures that mean the most to them.

"We no longer have God's beautiful trees and flowers outside our back windows," Elaine notes.

Instead, viewed from their new kitchen is what they call their "Cross Wall," housing four dozen unique artifacts artfully arranged around shuttered windows. The largest piece is an old filigreed church window salvaged from the front door of the small Pennsylvania town church where the seeds of Elaine's faith were planted as she grew up.

Other items were gifts or religious remembrances from the couple's travels and mission service, including crosses and angels from Peru, Mexico, Italy, Germany-Oberammergau, Colombia, Haiti, Dominican Republic, and more. There is a bright orange cross, hand-crocheted by a handicapped woman in Travis Park near their new home and a treasured photo of Mike with his son Matthew, who died at age twenty-one. There is a framed ceramic sun that their son Gregory made for Mother's Day when he was six years old, and next to that, a wooden "I Love Jesus" plaque that another son,

Marquez, made when he was in Bible school. There's also an angel from the Loretto Chapel in Santa Fe where Marquez and his wife shared with extended family a blessing of their marriage vows that had initially been exchanged abroad.

"There is a loving part of our lives in each of these 'keepers,'" Elaine adds, "and we love sharing the special significance when visitors ask."

Linda's Prayer Beads

Linda B's collection of prayer beads has been inspired by a variety of faith traditions. When her Roman Catholic relatives introduced her to their fifty-nine-bead rosary dating back to the fourth century, the idea of using beads as a prayer tool appealed to her.

"I have trouble keeping my mind directed and focused," she shares, "so to have something tactile was a help to me."

Later, she discovered the Anglican rosary, which was

developed in the late twentieth century. Its total number of thirty-three beads, she learned, represents the number of years that Jesus lived on Earth. Her brother-in-law, a Muslim, gave her some Muslim prayer beads, and a friend added a Buddhist set to her collection. She also became interested in beading as a craft, making prayer bracelets, many of which she handed off to people who admired them. Others slipped off her wrist amidst the hustle and bustle at airports and other places.

"I've lost more of those bracelets than I care to count," she says, "and I think maybe they've fallen someplace where they needed to go. Sometimes people just need something to hold onto if they're stressed or in trouble or anxious."

Even more, the beads, in all their various permutations, symbolize for Linda a belief that she's come to embrace as her understanding of various world religions grows.

"They remind me that while there are many different ways to express faith, we're more alike than we are different," she notes. "We want peace; we want harmony; we want to get along with each other. We just come at it from varied perspectives. Although the beads all look different, they are still a prayer aid for all of us."

Praying in Color Sketchbook

In the fall of 2012, I started wondering if God was getting a headache from hearing my repeated prayer requests. Was I asking too often for the same old things? Was I even getting through? Then Sybil MacBeth's book *Praying in Color* introduced me to a meditative and playful prayer practice that helped free my worries and offered a fresh start. It inspired a sketchbook of colorful doodles that have nothing to do with drawing talent (thankfully, at least for me) and everything to do with relaxing into effortless communication with a higher power who is wise, gentle, compassionate, loving, and kind enough to understand.

My sketchbook's pages hold various types of entries. On some, there is just one person's name decorated with a multitude of colored pencil markings as I hold that person close to my heart. Other drawings blossom from a particular word—the word "wait," for example—that resonated with me from a Bible passage. Others capture conversations or musings or mysteries to be unraveled.

The sketchbook reminds me that God is never too tired/bored/overworked/busy to listen and that no matter what approach the Holy Spirit inspires, there is always a way to connect.

Ten Years of Counted Blessings

When Missy's husband, David, was struggling with cancer, their lives were in turmoil. Not only did the uncertainties brought on by illness plague them, but the income from David's private practice business also came to a halt.

"It was the worst time of my life," she recalls.

During that period, Missy's mother gave her a journal called *Counting My Blessings*. Its pages invited her to write down five things for which she was grateful each day, and that is exactly what she did from 2002 to 2012. The journal, which, she says, merely lists day-to-day occurrences, illustrates the power of simple acts of gratitude.

"It is a priceless account for me of God's goodness in the face of tribulation."

Notebooks of Quotes

As we sit over tea at Linda B's kitchen table, she is leafing through pages of notebooks, in which she's collected bits and pieces of inspiration—"anything that speaks to my heart," she says—for what "feels like hundreds of years."

"This is so disorganized," she says. "You can see what a mess this is." Occasionally, she catches a scrap of paper slipping onto the table.

Her initial entry in the first of several journals was a Shakespeare quote, "To thine own self be true."

As she flips through, reading some passages aloud, she chuckles over their random nature and variety of sources. Scripture, a poem by Wendell Barry, Mark Twain, a sign on Route 222, a plaque she saw in a shop, a tear-off calendar page, Eleanor Roosevelt, Mother Theresa.

"Dr. Seuss: 'Don't cry because it's over; smile because it happened,'" she reads. "Mahatma Gandhi: 'There are people in the world so hungry that God cannot appear to them except in the form of bread.'"

My friend, widowed in her late fifties, notes that funerals can be a source of meaningful quotes. Others that she collected decades ago bring her back to the days of young motherhood.

"Some of them I can't even read without crying, because they're so moving to me," she admits. "You know, when I think of my children as infants."

Her eyes well with tears as she shares examples, ending with one from Charles Dickens: "I love these little people, and it is not so slight a thing when they love us."

One page has a newspaper clipping attached to it, and she continues reading aloud.

"Dear Abby: 'The Ten Commandments of How to Get Along with People.' I obviously didn't read that very well." She cracks up laughing, a contagious laugh, even though there's not a shred of accuracy in her self-effacement.

As Linda shares her special keepsakes, it occurs to me how much we learn about others through what inspires them and what a gift it is to be able to do so.

CHAPTER SEVEN

Home & Work

"I live in my Joy Chest."
—Jim

A cosmetologist for fifty-five years, my hairstylist Paula S. sprouted her wings in a beauty salon that her aunts ran. Her memory of business the way it used to operate is vivid.

"People would come in and get their hair washed, and they would get perms, and God only knows what products they used," she says. "They would get rollers and go under dryers. They would go home and put nets on their hair and sleep on whatever special pillowcases they could find. They'd spray with Aqua Net, and they would come in two or three times a week for a wash and set. It was a whole different world. Nobody did their own hair at home."

It was also a time when customers felt a keen sense of ownership of their regular weekly time slots. Paula recalls that, on occasion, a patron would arrive only to find an acquaintance still sitting in the chair.

"They would come over and stand right next to them and say, 'Were you late?'" she remembers. "And then they'd look at me and say, 'Were *you* late? Because this is *my* time. Why is she sitting here?' My aunts were used to it, but I kept thinking, something is wrong with this."

An artist at heart, Paula was struck by the lack of professionalism associated with her chosen career. But in the early 1970s, ten years after she'd started a successful salon of her own, a breakthrough approach to cutting hair, inspired by Vidal Sassoon, offered a whole new way of doing business.

Newly created shapes of the hair and training for customers to use products and maintain their own hair at home meant longer, but fewer, visits, now at four- to six-week intervals. An innovative team concept meant that one person would no longer do everything—cuts, color, nails, perms, make-up—and that professionals would specialize in different areas. The price for that less frequent and lengthier appointment would reflect the new level of training, service, and artistry.

"As soon as I heard it, I was like, 'Oh, my God, this is the way to go. This is like a phenomenon,'" Paula notes. "Now you look back, and everybody's done it. It's no big deal."

But in 1972, it *was* a big deal. In fact, the new ideas were so unheard-of—in the industry and with customers alike—that when Paula announced that she'd see her clients once a month or maybe once every six weeks, and that, with the new easier-to-manage cuts and products, she'd show them how to maintain their own hair in between, their response was "Oh no you won't." And her ten-year-old business took a nosedive.

"Everybody walked out. The whole staff walked out, the whole clientele left," she recalls. "I lost everything. I had gone to Sassoon's school and learned what I needed to do, and I was holding on by my fingernails."

Still, Paula was determined that the new approach was the right one. She hired another Sassoon-trained stylist, rounded up local college students willing to model the new cuts, did photo shoots, and contacted an area newspaper that ran an article featuring her maverick efforts.

After that, "it was like *boom!*" she says. "It was almost like I'd opened up a door and said, 'Over here,' and everything that was supposed to come in my direction did."

Her business, called Headlines III, grew and flourished. She'd taken a risk and was rewarded as owner of one of the most publicized and well-respected salons in the region. In 1978, she began running magazine ads that portrayed her clients, their careers, and testimonials, linking their professionalism with hers. The campaign, including dozens of full-page advertorials (advertisements that look like editorials), ran successfully for thirteen years. The cherished mementoes, now collected in a notebook, reflect the whole gamut of her clientele: entrepreneurs, media personalities, executives, educators, artists, volunteers, health care professionals, and many more.

"I look at the photos and each one makes me think, 'The best part of me happened that day,'" she shares. "I remember how comfortable the people were in knowing that they'd been cared for and the astonishing way that they were being recognized for who they were, what they did in life, and that somehow, we were gifted to meet each other."

One ad features a photo in which she posed with a pair of brothers who were well-known local entrepreneurs. Hand on hip, and dressed in a tailored suit with thin tie, Paula could easily pass for their business partner.

"I remember thinking, in the world I come from, I'm nobody, I'm just a hairdresser," she shares. "When I stood there with the two of them, I was a professional cosmetologist, and these two professional men were willing to stand by me and acknowledge that. It was really cool. And that's something that happened for each and every one of my staff. Employees got that they made a difference."

What does it mean to feel you are making a difference? For some, it means using your God-given talents to help fill the needs of others. It is a reminder that you matter. When the vocation you've chosen—paid or volunteer, in the home or out in the world—provides fulfillment, something clicks. Even with ups and downs, an underlying notion that "this is the right place for me" produces joy. The feeling is certainly there for Paula, now seventy-two, who, when asked how much longer she plans to continue her cosmetology career, replies, "They'll find me on the floor with the blow dryer going and a comb and brush in my hand."

In a similar vein, many people find a sense of belonging in the nest they've built, the style that reflects who they are, and the elements of comfort with which they've chosen to surround themselves. They cherish the family that makes a residence a home.

"I live in my Joy Chest," says Jim. "I have filled it with things that are loaded with memories."

For some people, home is where they first learned that they matter and within its walls, they found safety and perhaps encouragement. Among the photo albums that Karen plans to save is one documenting home, including mostly photographs of her current home, but also some of her parents' house, "places that make me feel secure and where I belong," she says.

Security, belonging, mattering, memories: It is easy to see why both the workplace and the home can be sources of joy. Here are a few more examples.

A Trophy and Letters

From 1963 to 1965, Ann taught at a secondary school in Ado-Ekiti, Nigeria, where she started a fine arts program. She calls her Peace Corps service there "the most important experience of my life" and felt privileged to teach some very talented students. Still, she was never quite sure if her efforts had made an impact on them.

Fifty years after she served in West Africa, she received the answer. A reunion for the school's graduates now living in North America was being planned in Orlando, not too far from her home in Naples, Florida, and she received an invitation. Her health was not good, so she responded that she was regrettably unable to attend.

Around the time of the scheduled event, she answered her door one day and, to her surprise, there stood some of her former students.

"You changed my life forever" were the first words spoken by one of them.

It turned out that Ann was the honoree selected that year, and her former students had come with gifts, a trophy, and various written expressions of gratitude.

"You remind me of a man who built a small hut in a village to cater for the needy," said one of the letters. "Years later…he wondered what happened to his former creation and found out that…it had transformed from a hut to a thatched house and then to a roofed house and now is a palatial edifice. By building a hut, he had built an edifice for the future. In the same way, Auntie Ann, you initiated a palace…from what you thought was the building of a hut…[and it] has turned out great artists of today that inundate the world with beauty.

"You deserve more than a trophy, Auntie Ann. Indeed, you deserve the world, for you changed our world in that corner of the earth. You created beauty in our space, you mentored initiatives in our lives, and you left joy in our hearts."

"It was the most wonderful moment," Ann shares a few days after her former students showed up at her door, "the surprise of my life. I hope you can understand why I have been shedding a few tears."

A Mother's Dining Room Chairs

When Jim was a little boy, almost seventy years ago, his mother purchased a set of antique dining room chairs.

It was a time when finances were tight for his parents, but he recalls the elegant dining room his mother created, complete with his grandmother's fine china and sterling silver pieces displayed in a glass-door breakfront.

"She was so proud to show off her chairs to her father when he visited from New Mexico," Jim remembers. "His only comment, which my mother always joked about, was 'they don't look bad for used furniture.'

"The chairs defined the room and anchored every holiday dinner, special occasion, and dinner party," he says. "I remember running around the table as a boy, holding onto the sculptured backs of the chairs as I did my laps."

As Jim grew, got married, and had children of his own, his widowed mother moved to a new home, where she still hosted family events at which the dining room chairs provided comfort and continuity. Eventually, she moved to a retirement community and, even though she had no dining room, insisted on bringing the chairs. After she died, Jim and his wife built a guesthouse behind their home where the chairs, along with other selected pieces, are displayed.

"Even today when I put my hand on the back of one of the chairs," he shares, "I'm flooded with great memories of my mother and times gone by."

A Bean and a Bag

Fifteen years ago, Barbara T. enrolled in a thirty-day program at the Kripalu Center in Stockbridge, Massachusetts, to become a certified yoga instructor. While there, she and her fellow students received what looks to her like a dried-out garbanzo bean. The token was to symbolize a seed that had been planted by their teachers to sprout and grow, spreading the fruits of all they'd learned. For years, Barbara carried the icon, tucked inside a small pouch, in her yoga bag as she passed along her knowledge in studios, workshops, and centers where she taught. More recently, she has also taken on work as a doula.

"Now I carry the bean in my doula bag because I don't always feel that confident," Barbara admits. "It gives me confidence."

Her yoga bag, a pinkish and gold-print hobo-style piece, is also one of her treasures. Purchased in Laguna Beach at the studio where she first taught yoga, the handmade bag holds her teaching supplies, such as poems, incense, inspirational phrases, and Tibetan chimes, and it accompanies her to all her classes.

"It represents fifteen years of teaching yoga," she says. "There's a lot of energy in it."

A Boss's Letter

When it comes to careers, some people recall with gratitude the person who first offered them the chance to prove themselves. For me, that person was Bob Kelly. I'd taken a clerical spot at his firm, Kelly Advertising, hoping to advance to a copywriting position. Based on a collection of unrelated writings I'd done—mostly college endeavors—Bob decided to give me a try at writing advertising copy. Five years later, I had built a portfolio of my projects, learned everything I knew about the business from Bob and his copy director, Phil, and moved on to an advertising position at a Fortune 500 corporation.

Soon after my departure from the ad agency, I was rummaging through my jewelry box one day. There, tucked in a compartment with a set of orange clown-shaped scatter pins I'd treasured as a little girl, my high school class ring, and the good-luck sixpence I'd worn in my shoe on my wedding day, was the classified ad that had first drawn me to Kelly Advertising. It offered the chance to begin with typing skills and then get into "anything you've got the talent and energy to learn." The headline was "START YOUR CAREER IN ADVERTISING." A wave of nostalgia and gratitude ran through me. Looking back, I could see that the promise in the ad had proven true. I attached the classified ad to a handwritten thank you letter, reminding the firm's owner of the first copywriting assignment he'd given me the chance to try. It was a product hang tag, a much-debated and revised project that had gone back and forth between the copy director and me.

"Poor Phil," I recalled. "Poor me! Poor, tired, lucky me."

I'd come a long way in those five years, and Bob Kelly had played a significant role in launching my writing career.

Soon after I mailed the note to him, I received a response. It began, "Gee, I suppose tough businessmen like myself should hate to admit it, but your letter did dampen the corners of my eyes a bit." He wrote that he'd read it to the entire team, wished me well in my new position, invited me to visit, and then, regarding my decision to move on from his firm, he added, "Please do keep in mind that if at any time you'd like to reconsider … "

It was a meaningful ending to an important chapter in my career.

My Mother's Meatballs Sign

Paula S. wanted to do something meaningful for her aging mother, Josie, so drawing upon her mom's experience as an Italian restaurateur, she devised an idea to package her mother's meatballs and sauce and sell them at a local farmer's market. Josie, at first, was not enamored with the concept.

"Are you crazy?" her mother exclaimed. "I'm too old for that!"

But Paula persisted. "You just have to sit there and look pretty," she asserted, planning to outsource the preparation of her mother's recipes. Thus, "My Mother's Meatballs" was launched, for which Paula commissioned a logo, labels, and signage.

The project lacked adequate funding to continue long term, but for the months it flourished, the mother-daughter bonding—symbolized for Paula by the logo and sign that still remain—was priceless.

"I wanted to do this for her before she passed away," Paula shares. "The stand was gorgeous."

And even more fulfilling for Paula was Josie's response.

"Oh, she was so happy," she recalls of her late mother. "There were tears in her eyes when people would come and hug and kiss her—people who remembered her pizza, her meatballs."

House Artwork

In 1972, Jim and his wife bought a 1785 brick farmhouse—their first and only house, which had no heat, electricity, plumbing, or closets. They worked on the dwelling for a year before moving in with their infant son, having completed only a kitchen and bedroom.

"Our lives have revolved around our home," Jim says, noting their shared interest in antiques, architecture, and art. Early on in the furnishing process, the couple purchased paintings from a local artist, Glenn Schlosser, also a favorite of Jim's parents. As a Christmas gift one year, his parents gave their son and daughter-in-law a Schlosser watercolor painted from a snapshot of their home as it looked when they'd bought it. The two were so enamored of the gift that they had Christmas cards made from the artwork to share with family and friends.

"The painting triggers over forty years of memories," Jim explains, "time spent restoring the house, directing the additions, planning the landscaping, acquiring antiques and artwork to furnish it, and most important, raising a family and living a happy life."

Grace and Gratitude

For more than thirteen years, Howard has facilitated writing workshops for various groups of women who have survived cancer. Participants are encouraged to freely express themselves, share their work, and engage in ten minutes of speedwriting based on a prompt that Howard provides. One group of four women has stayed together for the whole time.

"That's a lot of writing; that's a lot of sharing," Howard notes. "That's a lot of love."

After thirteen years, the women honored their facilitator with a gift they'd created as a tribute to him, a book entitled *Grace and Gratitude*. The preface thanks him for his years of dedication to the group, and Howard is quick to return the sentiment.

"I am grateful to them for giving me the gift of themselves and what we do," he says.

In addition to their photos, included in the book are writings from prompts that were most meaningful to each woman. The participants also enlisted the help of Howard's daughter to gather photographs of him with his late wife and others.

Replicating the "Ten Minutes of Speedwriting" exercise assigned at meetings, a section at the end is entitled "Ten Minutes of Speedwriting about Howard." In the entries, the women describe their writing coach as "a sensitive soul with a fun sense of humor," "wonderful mentor," "introspective," "deeply caring," "gentleman," "wisdom," "thoughtful," "our trusted leader."

To Howard, the book is a treasure.

"It helps to validate me as a human being, my 'mattering,' if you will, for it shows me that I certainly mattered to those people.

"From what I give, I get," he adds, "and the book reminds me of that."

An Oversized Matchbook

In 1984, Jim left a corporate position of nearly two

decades to partner with the founder of a local advertising agency. To announce the new partnership, the agency created a promotional piece in the shape of a giant matchbook. The cover introduced the firm's new name and logo, composed of the last names of both partners. The headline underneath: "The Perfect Match." Inside, the tips of die-cut matches featured portraits of the firm's nine staff members at the time. The announcement promised clients a results-generating combination of talents and noted that creative sparks were already flying.

"It marked the start of a happy and rewarding second career," Jim notes.

Decades later, the piece still holds meaning for him.

"The matchbook now unlocks fond memories of the special people I worked with, as well as the many notable experiences with a wide variety of clients."

Of the many keepers referenced in this book, the matchbook happens to be one that I've chosen for my own Joy Chest, as well. I can vouch for the fact that "The Perfect Match" proved true, as I was the partner whom Jim joined in 1984.

CHAPTER EIGHT

Creativity & Art

*"In my mind, I can still hear
the ballad's lyrics as I fall asleep."*
—Nancy

As Marion's vision has diminished from macular degeneration, so has her choice of activities. She is no longer able to drive or engage in the "hand arts," of which she was fond for many years. In February of 2016, the dark, dreary days of winter were upon her, and she was bored. But the nonagenarian is not one to wallow in self-pity.

"I decided, okay, I'm just needing something to stimulate me," she remembers.

Her out-of-town daughter had often expressed interest in Marion's stories about life in the early to mid-twentieth century.

"Almost every time my daughter's with me, which is not often," Marion notes, "she says, 'Mother, write that down.'"

It was this inspiration that put my industrious neighbor on the path to create a surprise Christmas gift for her children and grandchildren.

When I first got a call from her, informing me of her idea and asking if I'd be willing to edit what she wrote, I was puzzled. How could someone with severely impaired eyesight take on a writing project?

"Have you thought about *recording* your life stories?" I asked, thinking that I could help her do that and then my husband could transfer the recording to CDs.

But the former home economics teacher insisted, understandably, that writing gave her more flexibility in collecting her thoughts. Although she admitted her inability to read her own writing, she had "a helper who's pretty good at deciphering it." Marion would write the best she could, and Karen would transfer her thoughts onto paper in longhand for me to edit. My husband, a graphic designer, agreed to design the cover and interior pages with photos included to complement her stories, and then we would coordinate the printing for her. She figured it would take her about three months to complete the project, which she estimated at three or four pages long. A little less than a year later, we were rushing the thirty-two-page typeset booklet to the printer to be ready in time for Christmas.

Throughout the process, Marion expressed concern

about the idea seeming presumptuous, but after reading her rich and colorful stories, I tried to convince her otherwise. Most important, however, was what her family thought.

"The children were ecstatic," Marion recalls. "In fact, there was silence when they recognized what they were holding. I almost had to say, 'Stop reading, and let's finish Christmas!'"

An out-of-town niece, Marion's late brother's daughter, to whom she had mailed the gift, called to express overwhelming delight. Her father had died near the end of the girl's college career, and the stories my friend had recounted brought him alive again in ways that her niece had never before experienced.

Marion's family members weren't the only ones who found meaning in her project. For the ninety-two-year-old and her helper, Karen, who is twenty years younger and grew up nearby, the effort sparked lively exchanges.

"She was eager to talk about it," Marion remembers. "We had many interesting conversations that sometimes took us completely off our thought track, but it was a good thing. It was healthy conversation."

The creative endeavor also stirred Marion's sense of gratitude for her upbringing.

"We were not little goody-goods," she notes. "Oh no, there were kids' pranks." But the act of recalling her parents' kindness, compassion, generosity, and respect for others revived a sense of appreciation in her. Their example set the bar high for Marion and her brother, she noted, and she wouldn't have had it any other way.

"They never passed their adult issues on to us," she recalls. "*We* were their concern.

"Not to sugar-coat it, but our values were so instilled from early on," she adds. "If we were told that dinner was at whatever time, we *appeared!* The dinner table was a very, very valuable part of life. It was annoying when you didn't like the menu, and you had to sit there and wait until everybody was through enjoying it, and it was frustrating when your friends were sitting outside in the yard waiting for you—'*Hurry up! Hurry up!*'—but no, it was family time. I think we're missing some of that today."

On a drizzly spring day, at her kitchen table, Marion re-caps her work on the book. The Christmas rush is over now. Another winter has come and gone. Knowing the effort that went into the project, I ask, would she do it again?

"I'd latch onto it tomorrow if I could figure out what to write about," she enthuses. "It's a form of mental stimulation. That was as much of the value in doing what I did, just the stimulation.

"I didn't intend for it to be an autobiography," she adds. "I wanted it to be about the times, the lifestyle, and have my children appreciate 'why are you doing it that

CREATIVITY AND ART

way?' or 'why are you going to spend that much?'"

And just like that, she segues into reminiscing.

"The first dress that I ever bought—since I was in eighth grade, I've shopped alone—I paid five dollars for," she gasps. "For a dress! 'Ohhhh, what's Mother going to say?' Can you imagine? Five dollars wouldn't buy the *buttons* today!"

Creative expression, in whatever form—writing, music, artwork, handcrafts—can result in cherished keepsakes for both givers and recipients, gifts that are handed heart to heart, from one generation to the next.

The act of sharing itself produces joy, and utilizing God-given talents to give of oneself continues the cycle of giving. Just as Marion's hard work delighted her children, who gratefully received it, she herself had garnered the riches of the remembering, the creating, and the accomplishment.

Creativity connects people, leaving memories in its trail. Imagine decades from now when Marion's children come across the thirty-two-page booklet that their then ninety-two-year-old mother so lovingly produced. They will hear her voice in its pages, recognize her character in the stories, remember who she was, and understand a meaningful part of their own history. They may even recall their delight upon first peeling back the brightly colored Christmas wrap and the way their mother tried to minimize the work's significance, because humility is a trait of hers.

It was no surprise that my research revealed artistic endeavors among the keepers that, for many people, trigger joy. Having shared in the honor from both the creating and receiving perspectives, I have filled my own Joy Chest with them. Perhaps the examples that follow will spark ideas of your own.

A Crochet Needle & Bag

On a crisp December afternoon, my friend Nuria, a Costa Rican native, and I are browsing through the Lancaster Heritage Museum's gift shop. A framed piece of *scherenschnitte* catches my eye, reminding me of a late Dutch friend who was well known for her talent in this paper-cutting artistry.

"Isn't it neat how certain art forms can evoke memories of others?" I say, telling Nuria about Tilly and her *scherenschnitte* masterpieces.

"Yes," Nuria agrees. "I still have my mother's crochet needle and bag. She was crocheting when she died."

Her mother was making squares to be sewn together into a bedspread, which a cousin later finished.

"When she got up from crocheting, she had the heart attack. Those were the last things she touched."

A Child's Drawing

Now a college student, Joyce's great-nephew Michael has his sights set on textile design. From the time that he was four years old, he loved to sketch and draw. To this day, Joyce has kept one of his early stick figure drawings.

"It has so much more detail than what a normal stick figure would have," she notes. What she especially treasures is the memory that the artwork evokes.

"Oh my goodness," she remembers telling the little four-year-old as he drew, "you're doing such a good job!"

"Well," he answered without hesitation. "I've been doing it all my life!"

A Pillow Called "Pete"

Of the many needlepoint projects I've completed through the years, one that holds special meaning to me is a pillow called "Pete." Named by the canvas designer, he is a whimsical spotted blackbird dancing against a bright yellow background. At the center of the creature, a bold red heart emerges from a lop-sided square of eggshell blue.

As I worked on the piece, I was teaching my older daughter to needlepoint. We were meeting every Tuesday, stitching and having lunch together. Each stitch, it seemed, tightened our relationship. When I look at the finished pillow, my heart—like Pete's—bursts with joy.

Music for Memory

Paula P. speaks of the important connection between music and memory.

When she was eight years old, she started taking piano lessons and later toyed with the idea of majoring in music, except that she didn't consider herself a performer.

"My family was very artsy—music or theater, whatever," Paula shares. "So it was always there."

She would eventually give one concert in Williamsburg, which she considers "a disaster." In her mid-thirties, she opened a studio in Virginia and, as a piano teacher, noticed how one child could easily grasp a concept that another could not.

"I think that experience started my whole interest in the brain and how we learn," she says.

To stimulate her own memory in future years, she plans to save professionally performed recordings of pieces that she once played.

"There will be nothing from that concert in Williamsburg," she quips.

A Mother Bird

One week after Mildred's fifth birthday, her mother died. After the funeral, her paternal grandmother stooped down to Mildred and her sister.

"Your mother's gone away," she said. "Don't ever talk about her again."

And no one did. It wasn't until Mildred was to be married that her father finally gave her photographs of her mother.

In addition to the photos, Mildred treasures a painting hanging in her bedroom. It shows a mother bird with outstretched wings sheltering her two babies.

"That picture," she notes, "tells me how it must feel to have the care and love of a mother."

A Daughter's Pig Art

When Jim's daughter was in grade school, she drew a large picture of a mother pig with her five piglets. She was unhappy with the final piece because it looked to her as though the mother pig was sitting on two of the piglets. So she crumpled up the drawing and stuffed it into her backpack to throw away when she got home. Jim's wife found the artwork, smoothed out the wrinkles the best she could, and had it framed.

"For years, I had the drawing hanging on the wall in my office to remind me of my daughter and the drawing's near-death experience," Jim shares. "Upon my retirement, that drawing has a place of prominence in our bedroom and in our hearts."

Though Anne, now in her thirties, remembers being both embarrassed and surprised by her parents' action, Jim adds another perspective.

"I suspect that deep down she was pleased to see how proud we were of her, even if we all realized it was not her best work."

Fiber Arts

Decades ago, the intricate handwork of a dresser scarf set inspired Joyce to take up embroidery. As a young girl, she'd admired the coordinating pieces at her grandmother's house and decided to create a dresser scarf set of her own. The creation, which she still has—one large scarf and two smaller ones—launched decades of creating "all kinds of things," including smocking, needlepoint, rug hooking, quilting, knitting, and embroidery.

"My Aunt Mary gave me a book published in 1898 of all the embroidery stitches," she recalls. "It cost ten cents."

Joyce also treasures the first rug that she hooked in 1979. Its design features a rose, the favorite flower of her late mother.

"Rug hooking became quite a passion for a long time," she notes. "When I was doing it at the beginning, I kept very thorough records of what I used and how I dyed the material and how much it cost."

She saved the list and accompanying photos of her finished projects in case repairs were ever needed, but today the list has become a keepsake, a reminder of years of work that fed her creative spirit and filled her with a sense of accomplishment.

A Lullaby's Lyrics

When Nancy was a little girl, her mother used to sing her a Welsh lullaby.

Now at age ninety and under hospice care, she still recalls the ballad's lyrics as she falls asleep.

One day, a harpist named Cass, who was making the rounds, stopped into Nancy's nursing home room and, upon request, played and sang the beloved ballad for her. Tears of joy streamed down her face as the music brought back the memory of her mother's voice.

"She was a loving mother," Nancy recalls. "I can still feel her arms around me."

She is quiet for a moment, and then she grins. "Of course, we were all perfect children."

As Cass played the harp and sang that day, she was unsure of some of the lyrics, so Nancy wrote them down for her and kept a copy for herself.

"Sleep my child and peace attend thee
    all through the night.
Guardian angels God will send thee
    All through the night.

Soft the drowsy hours are fleeting
Hill and dale in slumber steeping.
   I my loving vigil keeping,
        All through the night."

Over the Christmas holidays, eight of Nancy's nine grandchildren came to visit her and to say good-bye. She had Cass come to play the harp for them, shared the meaning behind the song, and passed the lyrics onto her grandchildren.

"They left singing it," she says, smiling.

The Written Word(s)

An old high school friend recently reminded me of a file cabinet where I used to store—in alphabetical order—the stories and poems I'd written.

"You were my only teenage friend who had a file cabinet," she teased.

Certainly, my Joy Chest will include my own selected writings, not just for organizational purposes but also because each of them brings back people or places or experiences or ideas that mattered deeply to me. For weeks and months, and in some cases, years, I tried to capture thoughts that seemed to have wings, while at the same time letting go, hoping they'd find their way to kindred hearts.

In the process, I've learned to appreciate life's contradictions—for example, that the depths of loss can sometimes help us discover the heights of joy; less really can be more; and, if we honestly look within, striking similarities may exist with those whom we push away. My writing has also shown me that while some people may disagree with our beliefs or misunderstand our feelings, there are others who nod and say, "I know what you mean" or "thank you for articulating exactly the way I feel."

Joy Chest: Treasures for the Journey Ahead is among the books, essays, short stories, and poems that I will save in my own Joy Chest. It reminds me that the way we live life now is a preview of the richness we'll experience as years go by. The investment we make in relationships, the degree to which we stay true to ourselves, the experiences we create, and the ways we nourish our souls are all sources of everlasting joy.

Today's meaningful moments, I've found, are gifts that can be unwrapped over and over again throughout the years. Listening to others describe what matters to them has deepened my perspective on all that there is to appreciate in this life. For me, the privilege of gathering the stories of others and sharing them has made this book—their book, our book together—a veritable Joy Chest in itself. I am forever grateful.

CREATIVITY AND ART

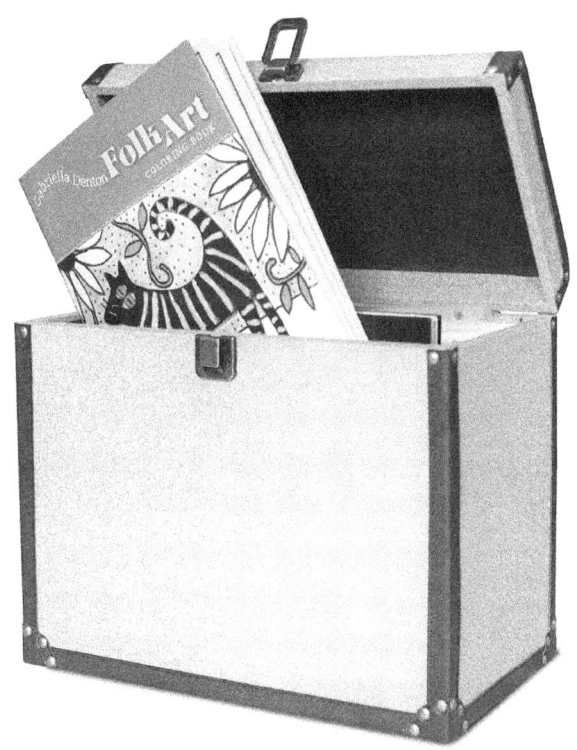

My own Joy Chest
and the treasure that inspired it.

Notes

1 Red Steagall, *Ride for the Brand: The Poetry and Songs of Red Steagall* (Fort Worth, Texas: Texas Christian University, 1993), p.79

2 UMNCSH (The Center for Spirituality and Healing), dir. "Brene Brown on Joy and Gratitude." YouTube. 28 November 2012. Web. 2 April 2018.

3 Cheryl L. Rice, "Welcome to the World," philly.com, September 3, 2013. http://www.philly.com/philly/opinion/inquirer/20130903_Welcome_to_the_world.html#TboV0VriV5TIUiVJ.99

4 Psalm 56:8, New Living Translation (NLT)

Acknowledgments

On my desk sits a miniature wooden chest. The five-inch-long replica was a gift from my friend Joyce Schroeder. It reminds me of the encouragement she provided for me to write this book, as well as the joy that her friendship brings to my life.

Through sharing pieces of their lives that they deem especially meaningful, the book's contributors—some whom I've known for many years, others who are new friends—have given this project life. My deepest gratitude to: Ann DeSimone, Barbara Templeton, Barbara Wiegand-Long, BJ Hamp, Cheryl Rice, David Marks, Elaine Dagen, Guy Guerriero, Howard Rice, Jim Corrigan, Joyce Schroeder, Karen Peckham, Linda Bruce, Linda Hatfield, Marion Gotwalt, Marissa Latshaw, Michael Latshaw, Mildred Lorch, Missy Deibler, Nancy O., Nuria Brenes, Pam Lazos, Patti Cornelius, Paula Porter, Paula Severino, Suzanne Wentley, Tony Baleno, and Ward Latshaw.

My friend and former business partner, Jim Corrigan, offered valuable feedback about research and early shaping of this book. He is a master problem solver with endless generosity, and I am grateful for his help.

Chris Noel, my editor, asked the right questions, shared insightful perspectives, added literary white space, and finally convinced me of the merits of the serial comma. Thank you, Chris.

Special thanks to graphic designer and illustrator Randy Groft and to photographer Katherine Groft for their generous sharing of artistic talents.

I am most grateful for the love and support of my family—Randy, Darcy, Katherine, Scott, Ruby, and Macy. They are my most cherished "keepers."

www.ingramcontent.com/pod-product-compliance
Lightning Source LLC
Chambersburg PA
CBHW022117040426
42450CB00006B/742